THE
CHILDFREE
ALTERNATIVE

Kate Harper

THE
CHILDFREE
ALTERNATIVE

The Stephen Greene Press
Brattleboro, Vermont

This book has been produced in the United States of America. It is designed by Douglas Kubach, and published by The Stephen Greene Press, Brattleboro, Vermont, 05301.

LIBRARY OF CONGRESS CATALOGING IN PUBLICATION DATA
Harper, Kate, 1946–
     The childfree alternative.

     Bibliography: p.
     1. Childlessness—United States.   2. Married people—United States—Interviews.   I. Title.
HQ536.H32   306.8   80-10593
ISBN 0-8289-0368-9

Without the people who willingly let me into their lives and consented to publication of their stories, this book would not exist.

Without the people who encouraged me, believed in me, and loved me, this book would be only an unrealized dream.

Thank you—all of you—for helping me to realize this dream.

Contents

Preface

A FEW YEARS AGO, I was around thirty, I hadn't had any children, and I began wondering what my life would be like if I never had any children. I wanted to talk to some people who didn't have children and find out how they felt. I looked for a book that might help, something I always do when I'm trying to learn about the world, and found nothing that satisfied my need for information. That is when the idea for this book was born.

My hope is to give you some information about how and why and in what context people decide not to have children. To make intelligent, well-thought-out decisions, we need as much information as we can assemble. Much of that information is our knowledge of our own feelings, thoughts, beliefs, and values. And we can also use the experiences and insights of others. We can see what in our experience is similar to theirs and what is different. Drawing from what we have in common with others and what we know to be unique in ourselves, we can decide which way to go.

I hope the stories of others who have decided against having children will be helpful to you, whether you are a young adult trying to make a decision about parenthood, a person who has decided to remain childfree, or a parent trying to understand why your child says she or he doesn't want to have children.

I'm reminded of some words my father wrote to my mother when he gave her the *Boston Cooking School Cookbook* shortly after their marriage. He was a sensitive man, and the implications of giving a cookbook to a new bride were not lost on him. He inscribed it, "As a help, not a hint."

I've always remembered those words, and they come to mind now, as I present this book to you. Like most writers (and some new husbands) I don't want to be misunderstood. And, like that long-ago cookbook, this book contains only some of the many possible recipes. Life is a matter of taste. We each have our special preferences among the many delightful and sustaining recipes for living. Take what you find here and elsewhere. Write your own.

One last word: the subject of this book invariably raises the issues of population, ecological balance, economics, and social change. Each of these areas is worthy of focus; to even begin to do them justice would shortchange the intention of this book. That more people are considering forgoing parenthood is, however, a part of and a result of massive social change. When an overview of those changes has been necessary, I have included such an overview. I have chosen to sacrifice comprehensive analysis to consistency of focus. The bibliography includes selected titles for anyone who would like to pursue some of the social and ecological questions raised here.

Here is my book, then. I offer it "As a help, not a hint."

Kate Harper
Moretown, Vermont

Introduction

1

Why This Book?

DECIDING WHETHER TO HAVE children is a complex, uniquely life-changing decision.

This book arose out of my mixed feelings about having children and my desire to know more about life without children. I had often said, half jokingly and half seriously, that although I wasn't sure I wanted many years of responsibility for a child, I would like to have grown kids someday. I seemed ideally suited to be a professional aunt.

I saw that wanting grown children someday was another way of saying that having had children might become more important as I grew older, hardly a good enough reason for having children. I was also intrigued by the question, What happens when people look back on their lives and their decision not to have children? I felt a need for some understanding of what that decision means to the people who have made it.

Who were some of those people? What kinds of lives did they lead? I wished I knew lots of people who were childless by choice, people who would tell me their thoughts and describe their feelings. I longed to ask them how they had come to be adults without children.

I couldn't think of more than one or two childfree people I

knew well enough to ask—and had they made a conscious decision? Perhaps they were unable to have children. I decided to
write this book and *find* people who would talk about choosing
to be childfree.

While I was working on the book, everyone who learned
about it expressed interest. Some people who had not had children and were still considering it said, "Maybe we will wait
until we have read your book. We don't think we want to have
children, but everyone who has them says we should." Several
people who had decided not to have children said, "Maybe
your book will help us feel less lonely and less like oddballs.
The worst part of not having children is that almost nobody
else you know has made the same decision." A few people said,
somewhat in jest, "I can hardly wait 'til the book is out. Then I
will be able to find some good excuses for not having any of the
little buggers."

When I talked to people with children, I heard several reac-
tions. One was great interest. "I wonder sometimes what my
life would have been like if I hadn't had any kids." Or, "I've
often wondered why people decide not to have children."
Sometimes they expressed disbelief. "I can't imagine anyone
living without kids. They are such an important and wonderful
part of our lives. I mean, isn't that what life is about?" Sometimes, rarely, they were hostile towards the idea of remaining
childfree. "Isn't that terribly selfish?" they would say.

Many people seemed to feel that not having children needs
to be defended. It is certainly a nontraditional choice, often a
misunderstood one. Sometimes, of course, it reflects a dislike
of children. More often, it reflects self-knowledge.

The key word, however, is choice. Having—or not having—
children is a choice. "You don't have to become parents, you
know," someone said to one of the couples you'll meet later in
this book. They began seeing that parenthood is an option.
Eventually they decided not to have children. No one told
them not to. Someone merely told them they had a choice.

We can ask almost any of our friends or relatives what having children is like, since most of them are parents. We were brought up in families; we know something about family life with children. But where can we find out how it might feel to have decided *not* to have children and to live with the consequences of that decision? Who ever talks about life without children? Almost no one.

A few years ago, Ellen Peck wrote *The Baby Trap*, extolling the virtues of the childfree life. Choosing to say little about what influenced the people she talked to, she stated the relatively obvious reasons they might have for wanting to remain childfree. They wanted freedom to travel, spend their money on themselves, or have time with their mate—and they weren't especially enamored of the prospect of having to care for children. They either weren't interested in or didn't like children.

The Baby Trap was a much-needed argument against the assumption that everyone wants or needs to have children. As such, however, it sounded anti-children and did not express any ambivalence about the choice to forgo children. When I think about never having children, I feel lots of ambivalence.

I also have some biases, and I might as well tell you what they are. I believe that those who have children should have them by informed choice. I believe that children are too precious to be created out of unquestioning acceptance of roles, expectations, or doctrines. I believe that simple failure to consider the alternative is no reason to have children.

I think that we have come to a significant crossroads in human life, one that may determine whether we will continue to be able to live on the earth. I think that those who choose to work on solving our enormous social, ecological, and moral problems are deserving of support, respect, and acceptance. If not having children is part of their contribution, I think we must respect that choice, even if we do not agree with it.

I believe that all of us are part of one family—the human family—and that all of us must choose our own way, fully aware that all choices involve some kind of loss. Finally, I believe that if someone simply doesn't want to have children, that's reason enough for them not to have any.

Deciding whether to have children is a momentous decision. For many of us, the longer we wait, the more complicated it becomes. For one thing, we settle into a certain lifestyle and wonder if we really want to start a family at the ripe old age of thirty-two. For another, this particular choice does not easily lend itself to purely rational decision-making techniques. Making lists of the pros and cons can help, but somehow that doesn't give us the information we need. Many of us feel that we must consider the larger social and ecological issues as well.

I'd like to share with you some of my thoughts and feelings, because those thoughts and feelings, stated or not, have influenced how I have approached the writing of this book.

When I think about never having children, I feel relief—and sadness. When I think about *having* children, I feel wonder—and fear. I doubt that I am unique. In either of these lives that I can choose, I will feel ambivalent at times. I know that. I'm still trying to figure out, if it is possible to figure such things out, which ambivalence I can live with more comfortably. But more than my comfort is at stake. Which path will help me to grow and develop into the sort of person I want to be? Which path offers the kind of life I think I want to live? Each offers both risks and rewards. Each is dangerous; each is uncertain. Such is all of life.

A sort of "Catch-22" surrounds the question of parenthood. If you have children and think they will be your ultimate fulfillment, you are destined to be disappointed. If you are capable of fulfillment in and of yourself, you don't need children. So if you are capable of leading a full and satisfying life without children, you are probably capable of leading a full and satisfy-

ing life with them as well. And if you can't fulfill yourself without children, having them won't help a bit. It may, in fact,
make your life more difficult.

One thing you can do is take a nice loving look at your life
and your self, that elusive person who has been with you all
these years.

I've looked at my own life and self; though I've found no
easy answers, at least I know what's there. I have opened all the
doors, so to speak, and what's behind them is not nearly as bad
as what I had imagined might be behind them. Some of my
fears are big ones, but I know what they are. I used four words
a while ago—relief, sadness, wonder, and fear. Let me tell you
what each of those words means for me.

Relief. If I never have children, I will be free of the incredible
demands of motherhood. I can write, travel, put my full energy
into my other commitments, whether they are to friends, mate,
community, work, or self. I can choose how I will live, where I
will live, without the responsibility of providing physical, emotional, and material sustenance for someone who is almost
wholly dependent on me. I can scrape by on little money and
lots of satisfaction in my work. I can have the time to do the
walking, the contemplation, the slow-paced living that my soul
thrives on. I can feel good about doing my part to ease the burden on social and ecological systems.

Sadness. But to never, ever, be a mother? The rest of my life
is a long time. Couldn't I give some of it, gladly, joyfully, for
the richness of an intimate relationship with a child? How sad I
feel when I think of never sharing in one of the most basic and
significant of human experiences. How terribly I feel the loss of
the child I'll never know, the self I'll never see and feel as a
mother. To grow as a parent is a special kind of growth that
may not be possible any other way. Do I really want to miss
that? Do I really want to miss knowing my beloved mate as a
father? How set apart from my friends and family I feel. How

painfully I feel the loss of connection to the rest of the family of humankind.

Wonder. What a wonder to create a child, to see myself and my mate reflected in his or her body, gestures, and values. What a wonder to live again—perhaps to resolve—some of my own childhood with my child, to rediscover the world through new eyes. What a wonder to watch myself as a parent, to respond creatively to the exciting unknown of my child. What a wonder, even, to see myself when I don't respond creatively or even rationally. I see parenthood as a special opportunity for expansion, for exploration. How few times in life are we called upon to be giving of ourselves when someone else needs us and not just when we choose to give?

Fear. The other side of the wonder is fear. Can I be giving on demand, for as long as I am needed? Will I resent those demands so much that I hurt my child? Will I lose the very things I most value about myself—my peace and radiance and joy? Will I go crazy with the unending responsibility? Will I be able to do everything a mother must do? Will I expect too much of myself and my child? Will I still be able to enjoy a full and intimate life with the man I love, or will motherhood replace being a lover and friend? I fear spending years of my life too tired to enjoy myself, my child, or my mate. I fear losing the time and space I know I need. I fear becoming too protective, too possessive, too demanding. I fear getting myself into the trap of needing to provide for my child and having to work at something I despise. I fear most of all that I simply don't know how a healthy family works and that I will collapse under the strain of trying to achieve one.

At times, it seems that both sides of the scale weigh about the same, and that is what makes this a tough decision, for me and for many other people.

I'm not positive that parenthood is wrong for me. But I must weigh the things I value most, what I want to do with my life, against what I sometimes feel I ought to want to do. And I certainly have felt, many times, that I ought to want to have children. I have even felt, at times, that I truly wanted children, that I would be a good parent and find pleasure and delight in my children.

Self-exploration, however, is not enough; the rest of the world is out there. We make this decision within the context of our society and our awareness of spaceship earth. Because we are faced with dwindling resources, population pressures, and human liberation issues, choosing to be a parent (or how many children to have) becomes a political act.

Because we have had the choice to remain childfree for only a short time, most young adults still follow a well-established route. They marry, or live together, have children, and see them into adulthood, so that their children in turn can do the same thing. It has almost an "as was and ever shall be" ring to it. For some people, this route is a fitting and necessary one if the human race is to continue. But not everyone can, or should, reproduce, if we are really interested in survival. This old world is going to run out of lots of things long before it runs out of people, even if many of us stop having children. Currently, only about five percent of all married couples choose not to have children.

Our society has absorbed many changes, some for better, some for worse; yet being an adult, especially a married adult, without children, has never been widely accepted or practiced among us. Making such a choice requires the ability to withstand many pressures to have children, pressures which persist despite our intellectual acceptance of the idea that people have the right to choose whether to have children.

For most of our early years, we're exposed to subtle and not-so-subtle messages to be fruitful and multiply. We're told that being childless is everything from unfortunate to immature, selfish, and unhealthful. No wonder it is often difficult for us

even to consider not having children. We suspect that something is wrong with us, that we just need to grow up and accept
adult responsibility, that we really ought to have children.
These pressures, referred to as *pronatalist,* are well-docu-
mented.

The pressures to have children are beginning to lessen,
though slowly. Our society more and more accepts choices that
allow individuals to live according to their own needs and
identities. I believe that all society benefits when people make
choices based on self-knowledge and information rather than
on expectations and ignorance.

At this point in our social evolution, the choice to have, or
not have children is more central to the lives of women than to
the lives of men. Women have been the primary care-givers for
children for all of human history. In many parts of the world,
women are now reaching out to take part in a larger range of
human activity. At the same time, the role of mother lingers
on as the true destiny of women. We have been told, early and
often, that our fulfillment will come from house, husband, and
children. It may, but then again it may not.

The women's liberation movement has not so much chal-
lenged our destiny as mothers as added to the definition of
fulfillment. Be a mother—and more—the workshops say. Many
women are working, marrying, and having children. They are
excited, proud, and tired. Being equal, for a woman, often
means being more. Many of us still feel that we must choose
between a demanding profession and an equally demanding
family life. But men have been able to have both. Some women
are asking, Must it always be this way? I don't think we necessarily have to choose between career and parenthood. I do
think that when we expect ourselves to be wonderful mothers,
dynamite career women, intimate marriage partners, and also
help run a household, we are asking a great deal of our time
and energy. We may be able, through superb organization, to

keep it all going. We may give up reading the books we'd like to read, taking the walks we'd like to take, and seeking the solitude we know we need.

But something has got to give. If we try to be super-women, the thing that gives is often our physical or emotional health. We find that a drink at the end of the day helps us relax. Then we find that one in the morning does, too. Or perhaps we see that our marriage is what is giving. Too bad, because we love our mate. Or we never seem to have enough time to spend with our children. Full-time work and full-time family life are difficult to maintain. Ask somebody who is trying to do it all. Most people will say they are paying quite a price for the privilege.

We need not, I think, resign ourselves to being childless career women or careerless mothers. We do need to be careful about trying to be all things to all people—including ourselves. We need to work at finding alternatives to a situation in which only women must struggle with how to manage being parents and workers and mates. We need to move towards a world of work that includes and encourages part-time career opportunities and not just part-time jobs. We need to push for child care where we work and where our men work.

Those of us who are of childbearing age today have inherited both the old expectations and the new freedom from having to conform to the old paths. Our options have expanded. Our needs and the world's needs have changed. We see that we can choose.

Making choices is a risky business. Not only do you sometimes explore unknown territory; if you get lost, you are responsible. Easier to let society, or your life, or your husband, take the rap. Easier to follow the well-traveled path than to break your own trail.

I am advocating a considerable amount of trail-breaking for all of us, men as well as women. We have come to a time when we can see where most of the old paths have taken us and where they will lead if we continue to follow them. We need not abandon them all. There is wisdom still in many of the well-trodden ways. But we are in need of new ways of exploring the territories opened to us through greater awareness and knowledge, greater capability for modifying our world— and possibly other worlds. Making choices, being responsible for our own lives, is exciting, challenging, and rewarding. In the midst of the many and complex social forces currently at work, we must be creative in using the fruits of our scientific, technological, and human-awareness explosion. May our human progress be as sound as our technology is prolific. May we weave the two together in such a way that our lives richen and deepen rather than merely expand in meaningless possibilities.

Mention of human progress suggests other good reasons for not having children. When I told Fred, my librarian-science fiction-fan friend, about this book, he pulled from his fertile memory, as he always seems to, just the right story: A contingent of Earthlings finally found their way to the right hand of God. The first thing they said was, "Well, you told us to 'be fruitful and multiply.' We did that. Now we are reporting for further orders."

That "be fruitful and multiply" business was sage advice when it was handed down, wherever it was handed down from. There was lots of land, but there were few people to live on it, work it, and enjoy it. All that untamed wilderness and no one to tame it; all that room, and no one to roam it. The earth seemed to go on forever. We know now that it doesn't.

Unfortunately, we have received no further orders—no stone tablets, no stars in the east, nothing. But we have the intelligence to make some decisions for ourselves.

I can also see and feel some good reasons for having children. I have come to understand that wanting to have children goes beyond purely logical arguments, beyond the need to perpetuate the human race. Most of us want to give and receive love, to feel that we are part of a continuing process, to witness and

nurture the miraculous growth from baby to child to adolescent to adult.

I really don't want to end. I know that some people say this
life is but a preparation for the next, that because we become
more wise, more peaceful, more aware, we are ready for death
and for what comes after. I have no evidence for or against that
belief. It would be a comfort to me if I could believe that this
life I cherish will continue in some form.

I really don't want the glorious Vermont Octobers to happen without my being there to appreciate them. Yet they will
go on, and I will not. The seasons will continue in their
magnificent indifference to my existence.

I feel sad to think of the world going on without me, just as
many people have felt sad. Is that part of the comfort of having
children? They will be there, when we are not, to smell the
flowers, to feel the rain on their faces, to stir the soup, to sing
songs. Someone will remember us with love. Some part of us
will move physically in the world. Yet the comforting thought
that my children would be here to carry on when I am gone is
little more than a sort of whistling in the darkest places of the
cosmos. My life will end.

A few people, a very few, feel completely at peace with not
having children. Most, however, wonder if they will feel the
same way as they grow older.

Sometimes when I see my friends with their little children
and see how rich the love that flows between them is, I wonder
how I could even consider missing what they have. Children
are bright, curious, lively, natural. For a brief time, we see human life without artifice. Children laugh, they cry, they learn,
they move, unselfconsciously. The parents are tender, atten-
tive, giving, understanding the needs of their children.

But that is a hopelessly romantic and simple picture of parents and children. The reality of being a parent is more than
the moment when you are joyously beholding your curious
toddler discovering a new skill. Being a parent means giving a

great deal of time, energy, thought, and resources to your children. There's more cooking, cleaning, shopping, loving, the more people you have in any household. Many people have children, enjoy them, feel enriched by taking care of them. But will you? That is the question.

After looking at themselves and at the social issues, some people have decided to stay childfree. They are what this book is about. The book speaks about the forces, personal, familial, and societal, which cause people to think that having children is a question of when, not *if*. The next chapter talks about some of those forces directly. The interviews that make up the bulk of the book talk about those forces through the people who have experienced them, thought about them, and made a decision not to have children in spite of them. They offer a look, from the inside, at what it is like to be an adult without children.

This book won't give you fifty good reasons for not having children. It won't tell you you'll be happier if you don't have any. It won't say that being childfree is morally superior. It offers no quick method for determining whether your decision about having children is consistent with your other goals in life. Only you can know that.

This book *will* give you a chance to meet some childfree people and find out how and why they chose to have no children. It will raise some issues you may not have considered. It will give you another view of some issues you have considered. And it will let you see that deciding not to have children—like consciously deciding to have children—is a complex process for most people. How they reach that decision is often as important as why.

We can choose only a few from the multitude of places to go, people to love, ideas to explore, and things to create. We can't do it all, thank goodness. Such limits make our choices more precious, our lives richer.

2

Why Do People Have Children?

NOT SO LONG AGO, no one asked why people had children. Women who married even twenty years ago didn't question whether they would become mothers. Children were a part of marriage. Many young adults today, however, are asking themselves whether they should have children. At the same time, their parents are expressing a desire for grandchildren. They might say something like this:

I've had kids in my life for the last twenty-nine years. It's hard to imagine a life without them. They were wonderful to have around, even though it was very trying at times. I never seemed to get enough peace and quiet, and there never was quite enough money. But we all made it, and now they are out on their own; it is just a joy to know they are in the world. I still feel a thrill when they come home to visit, and I look at them and think, except for Jake and me loving each other and bringing those children into the world, Susan and Little Jake and Robert would not exist. And that thought fills me with wonder. I mean, I'm just an ordinary person, but there are those three beautiful human beings who exist because of Jake and me.

Well, now Susan is saying she doesn't want to have children, and I can't understand it. My three brought me more joy than I can begin to tell, and they still do. Sure, it wasn't all easy. But it was worth it. I

14

saw Jake as a kind and loving father, and he seemed to grow in ways that I never would have imagined. He was so silly and wonderful with the boys sometimes; I would not have missed seeing that for the world. But Susan says that is not reason enough to have kids. Well, I suppose not, but if you looked at everything that way, I wonder if you'd bother to get up in the morning.

Part of the reason I don't understand it is that Susan is such a loving, bright person. She'd be a wonderful mother, and I feel cheated that I won't see her that way. We're close now, but somehow I think it would bring us even closer if she had some kids. Maybe she would understand a little better how it was for me. I don't think children and parents can really understand each other until the children have had some kids of their own. Then they know what it is like, and they know that their parents loved them, even if they didn't always know what to do.

And I guess I have to admit that I don't want the family to end. We're here because people had kids down through the years, and it doesn't seem right to let it end, after all that being born and living and struggling just to survive. It's like it was for nothing.

Maybe Little Jake and Robert will have kids. I hope so, because I sure do want to have some grandkids to love and spoil a little and enjoy. It would be nice to have some kids in the family who weren't my responsibility.

Why should Susan be different? All my friends' children are presenting them with grandchildren. I don't quite know what to say to them when they ask about Susan and Roy. It's embarrassing. I keep saying, well, not yet, but I can't say that forever.

Having a family. That's what life is about, isn't it? What else is there that matters very much? You can go out into the world and have a career, but when you are all done, what have you got? Maybe a little more money. Maybe even you're famous. But that's pretty empty beside having your sons and daughters home for holidays once in a while and feeling again: those wonderful human beings exist because of me. Susan says that's just a lot of ego, a way to feel powerful. I say it is love.

What you just read is something I wrote after talking to parents and thinking about how I might feel if I had children who decided not to have children. I would feel pretty disappointed, especially if my own experience as a parent had been a reward-ing one. How could I begin to understand a decision that so totally negated, somehow, twenty or thirty years of my own life?

These emotions are an important side of a hard question. Emotions can't be refuted; they can only be felt. But how we feel, or how our parents feel, is only part of the basis for mak-ing a decision about parenthood. Unfortunately, we don't know very much about why people choose to have children, because most people in recent history didn't *choose*. They sim-ply had children. But why do people *now* have children?

When I started my research for this book, I went into a bookstore and asked for a copy of *The Baby Trap* by Ellen Peck. Besides finding out about why people have children, I wanted to read everything that had been written on the subject of choosing *not* to have children. Everything proved to be very little.

When the woman at the store asked me what the subject of the book was, I told her it was about voluntary childlessness. "Well, I think everybody should have at least one," she said, in such a way that I could not tell if "having at least one" was a source of joy that no one should miss or a duty that no one should escape. She went on to tell me how nice it is that there's no pressure these days for anyone to have children.

Relatively little research has been done to try to find out why people have children and how people in general feel about having—or not having—children. A few studies on the effects of children on couple relationships exist, and many people have researched and speculated about the question of maternal instinct. I read the literature to get a feel for what is known and what is yet to be discovered in these areas. I would like to give you the benefit of my reading with an overview of the research that has been done and the conclusions, if any, that have been reached. You may want to do some of this reading on your own and refer to the bibliography at the end of this book.

First, however, a little about the language hassle. Our language reflects a bias towards parenthood as a positive thing and childlessness as a negative thing. Traditionally, the word *childless* indicated an inability to have children. Until recently, when the word *childfree* came into use, people who decided to have no children were identified primarily by what they were not (*nonparent*) or by what they did not have (*childless*). *Childfree* retains some of that bias and is pejorative towards children.

Childfree. It *is* more positive sounding, but somehow it suggests that children are a bad thing that you are lucky to be free of. For some people, that may be accurate, but most of us feel otherwise. Childfree echoes other terms we use similarly, such as disease-free, trouble-free, worry-free, and carefree. I keep insisting that we must be able to do better than that, but so far I haven't come up with a good substitute. "Nonparent" is like nonentity and nonsense, although being a nonsmoker has a certain amount of status these days.

Even the National Organization for Non-Parents has changed its name to the National Alliance for Optional Parenthood, possibly as a way of seeking a more positive image. Language and attitudes are inseparable.

I generally resist the use of labels like Parent, even though I see the usefulness of naming some roles. No role, however, is the total person. People who are parents are far more than parents. People who are adults who do not have children are more than nonparents. All people have realms of their lives that have nothing to do with whether they have children. My own solution to the semantic problem is to use *childfree*, *childless*, and *nonparent* almost interchangeably and to avoid using any of them when possible.

What of the much-discussed "maternal instinct"? How does it affect the childfree alternative?

Whenever we look at human behavior, one of the big questions is: how much of what we do is culturally determined,

learned from other people? How much of it is innately part of
us, with us when we are born or built in as part of our growth?
No one knows the full answer, but researchers are constantly
trying to unravel this fascinating tangle.

Because all of us have been greatly influenced by our families, friends, and communities, by the time we are part of a
research study, we have added many layers of behavior, knowledge, attitudes, and feelings to whatever we were born with.
Therefore, we cannot merely ask a woman if she has a maternal
instinct. She might very well answer yes, because she has been
taught that certain feelings which she has experienced are
called the maternal instinct.

Until recently, an adult without children was often the ob-
ject of pity. People were usually childless because they were
unable to have children or because they couldn't find mates.
Relatively few married people made a choice not to have children. A person who chose to be childless was, and often still is,
scorned, misunderstood, and pressured to have children. Why
is this, and what do studies tell us about our attitudes and
ideas about having children?

At least seven commonly repeated themes concerning having children appeared in what I read. I choose to call these
themes myths, because part of the reason for any mythology is
ignorance. Until quite recently in human history, ignorance
about procreation was not too serious a matter, since people
didn't have much choice anyway. Today, choosing whether to
procreate is part of our lives. When stated positively these
myths were about parenthood. When stated negatively, they
were about being childless.

Myth Number One: Having—and therefore wanting—children
is natural. Most of us have been taught to say and to believe
this. The negatively stated side of this is that not having—not
wanting—children is unnatural. Somehow, when we start talking about having children, the word *natural* takes on almost
mystical meaning, as if naturalness is the ultimate test of right-

ness. Perhaps it is, but if we apply it to only one area of life, its meaning is completely lost. We have experienced such rapid technological and social change that we inhabit a world vastly different from that of fifty or even ten years ago. "Natural" applies to little in the human world we have created.

Whether wanting, as opposed to having, children is a natural part of our existence is an open question. We've all had so many messages about having children since we ourselves were children that it may be virtually impossible to say what is a true desire for children and what is a good selling job. Children used to just happen, wanted or not.

Myth Number Two: Women have a maternal instinct that needs to be fulfilled. The negative correlate of this one says that women who deny their maternal instinct will always feel that they have denied their essential nature and function. This is the same as saying that having babies is all that women are good for.

Most of us have been exposed, to one degree or another, to the idea that women have a natural, inborn desire for children, and a natural, inborn capacity for taking care of them. This idea, which possibly has some validity—thousands of years of evolution can't be totally ignored—makes women who consider the possibility of remaining childfree uneasy. If maternal instinct is mythology, its power can still persuade the hesitant to become parents.

Instinct is a tricky matter. Certainly we do those things that keep us alive as individuals; it might be possible to extend that and say we procreate out of an instinct to preserve humankind, to keep us alive collectively. Two things are clear. One, we sometimes can choose, without endangering our survival, to ignore those inner voices telling us to eat, to sleep, to mate. Two, being biologically capable of having children is different from wanting to have them or knowing how to take care of them. In any event, researchers have so far been unable to prove that a maternal instinct exists.

I think that a nurturing instinct exists in all of us, but it comes into being when someone needs us to nurture them. Ample evidence shows that fathers have that care-giving disposition just as much as mothers. But we simply don't know how much of that is innate and how much is learned. If maternal instinct proves to be more than just a pervasive social environment that compels women to become mothers, I will be surprised. Either way, the problems arising from going against that instinct are probably tied more to social pressures than to denial of an instinct. We don't know.

Myth Number Three: Children bring couples closer together—they make marriages happier and more stable. The negative side of this, of course, is that childless marriages are unhappier, more prone to break-up. Many studies have been done; all of them point to the same thing: marital satisfaction tends to decline with the advent of children. Being a parent brings a lot of satisfaction to many people, but that satisfaction often does not extend to the marriage which produced the children. Many people find that their marriages no longer seem very close. I'm sure that sharing parenthood with someone they love does bring some people very close. Even so, the marriage that includes well-brought-up children and is also a source of pleasure, growth, and contentment for both people seems to be quite rare.

A study, headed by Dr. Angus Campbell of the University of Michigan's Institute for Social Research, found that of all people, married and single, the most content were young couples without children. Next were older couples without children, and third were parents whose children were grown. The people in the study defined contentment in their own way.

More divorces occur within one year after the birth of a first child than at any other time. Many people have looked back on their lives and said that even though they love their children, if they had it to do again they would choose not to have children at all. As for the staying power of marriages, those with and without children tend to have about the same durability, although childless marriages may have a slight edge. The study results get a little cloudy because many marriages break up in the first few years, independent of whether the couple intended to have children later in the marriage.

The evidence suggests a really crucial issue: being a good and contented parent and being an intimate and contented mate are two different things. Being parents and being lovers require different skills and priorities; the two roles are difficult to maintain at the same time.

Children are an added stress for most couples. Those who decide to have a baby to save a failing relationship are, I'm afraid, sadly mistaken.

Myth Number Four: People who are parents are superior because of the sacrifices they make for their children. The negative correlate says that people who don't want children are selfish.

While being a parent does require the devotion of time, energy, money, and loving care to children, parents have brought their children into the world, created them, created the need for all that time and money and loving care to be expended. People who don't have children often give time, money, energy, and loving care to other people, to causes they believe in, and to meaningful work.

Parents probably have children because to do so will satisfy some of their needs and will allow them to live the sort of life they want to live. People choose not to have children for the same reasons. Both can be considered selfish.

Many things in this life require attention, love, care, and hard work. Being a good parent is one of them. Writing a good book, learning to play the violin well, being at peace with yourself and your world, also qualify. And yet none of us are accused of being selfish if we choose not to devote years of hard work to the violin.

Some people feel very upset when they see childfree couples

who are happy and contented. They may question their own choices. They may feel extremely jealous of the freedom they now realize could have been theirs, if only they had considered the options more closely. They may attack those people who did consider the options.

Myth Number Five: Having children is one of the necessary stages in adult development; people who have children become mature, stable adults. On the negative side—fulfillment is not possible without children, nor is maturity. People who don't have children are neurotic.

Many psychological theories have helped promulgate this myth, because they document the stages most adults traditionally go through on their way to old age. Because most adults were parents, we've been fooled into thinking that is the only way you can be a card-carrying adult—a normal adult, that is.

Parenthood is one kind of development. I cannot deny the importance of being a participant in the great human chain of being a child, then a parent, then a grandparent, to die having passed the torch of existence on to your sons and daughters and grandchildren. But many other kinds of development are possible and valuable. Each of us must choose our own way. We can lose sight of personal developmental needs if we get caught up in someone else's definition of what ought to make us feel complete.

People who are parents may or may not be stable and mature, just as people who are not parents may or may not be. Parenthood can push someone into accepting a more responsible role and becoming mature more quickly, or it can cause so much stress that child abuse or neglect becomes an ugly reality.

Some counselors have labeled their women clients immature or neurotic if they expressed the desire to remain childfree. Having children was sometimes seen as a cure-all for personal and marriage problems. I encourage counselors to work with their clients to help them discover and achieve what is right for them as individuals.

Myth Number Six: Children give you immortality and a purpose in life. The negative correlate says that not having children means the end of your family line, and gives you nothing to "keep you sane," as one friend of mine put it.

If you don't have children, your genetic inheritance *will* die with you. Yet having children does not guarantee that your genes will be carried forward more than one generation. Your children can choose not to have children. They can die before they reproduce; they can be sterile. How much does it mean to you to achieve genetic continuation, which may or may not happen anyway? Only you can decide.

As for purpose in life, I can't tell you what it is. I like to think we are here for more than mere physical continuation. We have wonderful capacities for things far beyond simple physical survival. To create other human beings just so we will have something to do doesn't seem quite right. What about their lives?

Myth Number Seven: People who are well educated, aware, and able to afford children should have them to offset the numbers of children being born to people who don't give it a second thought. On the negative side, this one says, that if only the well-educated, aware, solvent people decide not to have children, the future of our country, not to mention the gene pool, looks pretty dim.

Ironically, most of the people who make a rational decision not to have children are just the sort of people who make good parents. They are bright, self-aware, socially conscious, and able to afford kids. Some of the people who have the most children, and do the worst parenting, are merely letting nature take its course, blindly reproducing with no thought about either their own capacity to take care of them or the world's capacity to support them.

Remember that the number of people who decide to forgo parenthood is extremely small. It may be more important for a few socially conscious people to contribute their time and energy directly to the pressing problems that face us on a global scale. Too, those who are now choosing not to have children are important role models for people who may not now be aware of the alternative available to them. The use of birth control began as a middle class or upper class luxury, even though the poor needed it more. Now, all except the extremely uninformed are using it.

I think "information-poor" is the way to describe those who continue to have too many children. For some, one is too many. We all need information about our own power to choose, about alternatives, about birth control, about world resources. Only then are we truly able to make a choice.

I have talked to many people who have decided not to have children; most of them, I am sure, would have been very good parents. But I don't regret their lack of children. Many of those people are in their early thirties and have only recently felt a sense of constructive control and self-worth emerging in their lives. As many of them said, they might not have been able to get to where they are if they'd had kids. Maybe they became people who would make good parents by not becoming parents. They learned how to live their own lives first. Now that is something to think about.

What does all this tell us about wanting children, about what a true desire for children might be? Not much. It tells us something about popular ideas about having children. It indicates that having children is sometimes a response to a feeling that life is empty and meaningless, sometimes an attempt to salvage a shaky marriage, sometimes a result of pressure from other people.

Some people are horrified that anyone would even question why people have children. They say, "It is not something you question. You just do it." That is the way many people have their children. Why people don't have children is much easier to pinpoint than why they do. I don't pretend to understand fully why people want children. No one understands this fully.

Some irrational elements are at work when people feel a strong urge to have a child, despite their rational decision to not have children.

Wanting children means that you feel you have something good to offer to children; you are willing and able to make that a major focus of your life. Wanting children may mean that you have established a wonderful intimacy with your partner and a life that you now wish to share with another person. And it means much more.

New life is beautiful, and hopeful. But being a parent is a very special occupation. Not everyone wants to be a parent and not everyone is good at it. Those who feel no need or desire to have children can logically choose to remain childfree. What could be more absurd than to ask intelligent, thoughtful people who have made this choice to fly in the face of it and have children anyway because they will be missing something, or because they will regret it when they are older, or because, well, having kids is just natural?

And yet this has been said, by well-meaning friends and families, to many of the people who have chosen to be childless. They have been told to stop being so selfish, to make their parents grandparents. Instead of being commended for knowing their own minds, they are condemned for being self-centered.

In the best of all possible worlds, at least some of those who were most ready, willing, and able to be parents would have the children, while those who felt most capable and desirous of doing other things would do something else. It all needs to be done.

The people you are about to meet have found that they can love and be loved, give of themselves, without having children. For them, not having children feels right.

3

The Interviews

B EFORE I STARTED this book, I knew only one person who
I was sure had chosen not to have children; we hadn't
talked about her choice beyond that. When I was looking for
people to interview, I asked my friends to let me know about
people who might be willing to tell their stories. Almost everyone I asked said the same thing: "Well, I know a couple without any kids, but I don't know if they couldn't have them or
chose not to." A very few of my friends were aware of
someone's conscious choice to forgo parenthood.

Our lack of knowledge about childless people says several
things to me. While few of us know many people who have
chosen to remain childfree, even fewer of us know whether the
childless people in our lives are childless by choice or by
chance. Most of us, sensitive to the feelings of others, are reti-
cent about asking people whether they decided not to have
children. For one thing, it's none of our business. For another,
they may be unable to have children. Perhaps they feel sad,
embarrassed, frustrated. And so we don't hear much about
voluntary childlessness unless our friends choose to tell us
about it. Often, unsure of our response, they say nothing. We
stay uninformed—and curious.

The people you are about to meet are fairly representative of people who have chosen to have no children. They tell you here how and why they made that decision, or how they discovered that their decision was made subconsciously long before they were fully aware of it. They speak here to help you understand the process that made them choose not to be parents. They speak only for themselves, with the eloquence of personal truth.

"Interviews" is an inadequate word for the conversations I had with the folks who agreed to talk with me. Rather than ask a prepared list of questions, I encouraged people to tell their stories in their own way. I had a list of things I wanted to know, but rarely needed to use it.

The conversations usually lasted from two to four hours; sometimes we shared a meal, a bottle of wine, an afternoon of gardening, a walk in the mountains, a search for wildflowers. Rambling a bit, those conversations were usually about more than just the direct answers to "How did you come to decide not to have children?" and "How do you feel about that decision now?" The indirect answers have a lot to do with who the people are and what has happened in their lives. Seeing the whole picture helped me understand; I hope it will be helpful to you. I edited the interviews, rearranged things a bit when chronology was unclear, and retold, in my own words, some parts of these stories. But for the most part, you will meet these folks pretty much as I did.

As these conversations indicate, making a decision about whether to have children is complex. How we grew up, our family life, our parents, our dreams, our values, the events of our lives, all shape the way we approach this question. In fact, they determine whether we even see it as a question.

A certain person or couple chooses not to have children for a combination of reasons. Sometimes one reason is stronger than the others; sometimes they all have about equal weight. These reasons come together in such a way that not having children offers itself, after much soul-searching, as the best alternative.

Sometimes the decision not to have children becomes apparent after the fact. "I thought I was just putting it off, enjoying some time with my husband, but now I see that I was deciding never to have children," one woman told me. The fabric is woven over a span of years; the pattern appears only when you can see the warp and the woof together.

Almost everyone I talked to said, "There was no one time at which I said, 'I am not going to have children.'" Often, however, the realization did crystallize at a certain point.

The interviews are divided into two sections. The first is a group of conversations with couples who made a decision, together, not to have children. The second is a group of conversations with single women who didn't marry, or made the decision, alone, not to have children, even though they may have been married at one time. This section begins with a chapter on what I call the "thirties crisis"—being childless and undecided in your early thirties.

I didn't neglect the single men and the sixty-year-old married couples by design, but they are neglected. My methods for finding people to talk with failed to net single, childless men. Only one older couple agreed to talk with me; one woman in her eighties who had never married was happy to tell her story.

I began by asking friends to suggest people who might be willing to talk about being childless by choice. I then asked each of the people I interviewed to give me more names. I sent posters around to friends, asking that they put them up on community bulletin boards. I followed each lead, trying to make sure that I got as wide a representation of ages and backgrounds and lifestyles as possible. But no single men came forth.

I met many men in their thirties who had not yet had children, but they were unwilling to say that was a permanent decision. Some were living with women who had children.

I imagine that most older people are reluctant to talk about such a personal subject. Helen and Scott Nearing, who certainly can give a long-range perspective, told why they didn't have children together, but only Helen totally abjured having children—Scott had children in his first marriage.

I tried finding older people through the Foster Grandparent Program, but if any of them chose not to have children, they were not willing to discuss it. I must assume that very few married people who are in their sixties today made a conscious choice not to have children. Such a choice was almost unheard of thirty to forty years ago. I guess you had to stay single if you didn't want children.

And so, I give you the conversations, with one last comment. Whenever we try to pin down the truth, if we look at what we have said, we find that we have not quite told the whole story. Something we can't quite express always eludes us. Such is the stuff that poetry and paintings are made of. Our lives are mysterious, even when we can tell everything that has happened to us. Much happens in places we rarely see.

To preserve confidentiality for the people I interviewed, I changed all the names (except those of Helen and Scott Nearing) and a few identifying facts. Being childless is public information; having a vasectomy, an abortion, or an unconventional lifestyle, isn't.

I'm no believer in final answers, because change is constant. But I know that the people I talked with made an honest attempt to reveal all that they knew about how they came to be adults without children.

Married
Nonparents

4

Steve and Anne

I Like Tigers, Too,
but I Don't Live with Tigers

STEVE AND ANNE have been married for eleven years. Both are thirty-four. In 1974, after they decided not to have children, Steve had a vasectomy.

I had not met either of them before the interview, but when I called to ask if they would be willing to talk with me, their response was, "Sure! And come for dinner." I agreed to pick up Anne at her office one day after work.

When Anne and I arrived at their home in the country, Steve was home, and he had already cleaned the house and bought groceries. Both of them have jobs in town; both believe in sharing household tasks.

While Anne started making her "very special spaghetti sauce," Steve served us something cool to drink. I cut up several large onions for the sauce, and then while it simmered, we moved to the living room and explored together some of the strangeness of first meetings. Steve and Anne were warm, sensitive, and easy to talk to. They were interested in and encouraging of what I was doing and why I was doing it.

Although Steve and Anne both grew up in cities, the similarity of their backgrounds ends there. Steve, one of three children, was part of a working class, traditional family—his

32

mother stayed home while his father worked. They were Catholic, "but not very religious," and Steve attended parochial schools, including college. His memories of his family life and childhood are mostly happy ones.

Anne was an only child whose father, an engineer, died when she was ten. Soon she and her grief-stricken mother began feuding, a pattern that lasted for years. When she could, Anne went to boarding school to get out of the house. Her memories of family life and childhood before her father died are happy; later memories are often bitter.

Steve has a brother four years older and a sister fifteen years younger than himself. He used to babysit for his sister a lot, and "that played a big part in my decision not to have kids. I enjoyed it, but once was enough." He started working with kids when he was sixteen, first at a day camp and later at a day-care center.

His older brother has two children. "That took the pressure off." Steve felt that his parents would make wonderful grandparents, and was delighted that his brother had children. He has told his parents that he is not going to have kids, but they don't know about the vasectomy. Their attitude has usually been broad-minded: "If that is what he wants, fine, as long as it makes him happy."

Steve, who likes himself most for his "warmth, compassion, and sincerity," says, "My love for children expresses itself with other people's children. I want children in my life, and that satisfies it for me."

Anne says, "I was very happy until I was ten. I was not brought up to be a girl. It was *when* you go to college, not if."

Almost all of Anne's sixteen cousins have children and live in the suburbs. But her mother has broached the subject only once and has not pressured Anne to have kids, probably not the usual scenario when an only child decides to stay childfree.

Anne always took it for granted that she would have children one day. But the women's movement made it easier for her to make a decision for herself instead of conforming to expectation.

Steve, too, says that the women's movement may have had some influence on his decision not to have kids. "It frees people." He became aware of the greater self-confidence of women in the last decade, a self-confidence that opened greater possibilities for men. "Women were saying they could take control of their lives. The women's movement has had a very fine and profound effect on my life. I now feel the courage to be myself and not live according to the expectations of others. As Anne has come to be able to experience her whole self, I have been able to also."

What does Anne appreciate most about herself? "I'm a very loving person; I have a lot to give and I'm not afraid to show it. I love my friends, and I'm not afraid of adversity."

At this point, Steve thought of another of his qualities. "I like my sense of humor." Anne added, "Yes, he has a strain of nuttiness. He also has a knack for sincere interest in other people. He is warm, spontaneous. People feel good about themselves around him."

Anne told me, "We try to have an egalitarian relationship. The cooking and cleaning are shared—but he does the heavy stuff. We do a lot of work together."

They have felt no condemnation from other people. They have felt misunderstanding. "People don't understand that you can love and enjoy children even if you don't want any of your own." They have friends who have children and love some of those children dearly. Steve jokes, "I like tigers, too, but I don't live with tigers."

Both Steve and Anne grew up thinking they would have children—it was just part of life. But when Steve admits, "At this point in my life, I could live with it if we had a child," Anne's answer is short and emphatic: "No!"

How did these two people decide, together and separately, not to have children? What events in their lives influenced that decision? Steve spoke first.

"I always thought I would have kids. It was something that was just accepted. I never thought whether or not I wanted them, I just thought I'd have them. Then when Anne and I were married, we talked about having children, and I guess I was more negative then. I said that was something I would never do. But then again, I was the kid who had always said, when people asked me when I was getting married—'two years after the Pope.'

"I can't say why I didn't want to have children. I was very young then, in my early twenties. I guess I didn't want the responsibility. It seemed like an overpowering responsibility.

"I had worked with children since I was sixteen. I'd seen a lot of kids who were in trouble. There seemed to be a lot of them; it would have been better if they had not been born. They were children who had just been beaten down by living in the city, poor. It scared me.

"And I thought that it's really hard to raise a kid without creating some sort of trouble for them. I didn't want to be in that position. I guess that is what I was thinking of when I said then that I didn't want to have children."

But Steve's strong fears about having children changed. "Later I realized that I could be a good parent because I was good with kids. But there were other things I wanted to do with my life. I wanted to remain pretty free not to have to succeed in traditional ways, not buy into that old way of life that I saw as very repressive and very closed. People get married and they have kids and spend the rest of their lives working in order to support a family.

"When I first started getting serious about Anne, I said to her, 'I don't know where I'm going with my life and I don't know what I'm going to do. I haven't any large ambition. And it may be a rocky road. I don't know where it is leading, but I'd like you to travel with me.'

"I guess that has been one of the themes of my life. I don't know where it is going. I'm willing to live it as it comes. And bringing another person into that was not fair I felt at the time.

Not fair to me and not fair to that person. I guess I still feel that way. I haven't settled into a profession. I was teaching for seven years, but I didn't want to do that for the rest of my life. I guess not having children has allowed me to keep my options open. Not having a child allows me to say that if this doesn't work, I'll just sell the place and maybe go back to school, maybe travel, maybe write. The options are open. The decision is mine.

"I have only one other person to account for, and that's Anne. But she is her own person, so I account for her only insofar as I love her, not because we have so many people to take care of.

"Our relationship is stronger because we've only had each other. It would be very easy in the economic sense for us to break up. The only thing that keeps us together is the fact that we have a continuing love affair. I think children would have altered that. Maybe for the better—I don't know. I think we've stayed younger, to some extent, because we're open to change, open to growth. And we look to each other for support. I think that has strengthened the bonds between us. I think we are each able to stand alone, but choose to stay together."

Anne's agreement is complete: "Absolutely," she says.

Steve continued. "I don't know how much of the decision not to have children is tied up in a negative feeling about yourself. I know for a long time, until very recently, I had a fairly deep negative feeling about myself. I think not having children—and I'm not saying this can't happen with children—allowed me to work through a lot of that. I'm at the point now where I pretty much like myself. I give myself permission to be happy, to take care of my own needs. I think if I had focused on a child, I might have submerged those needs. I'm glad I got an opportunity to work through that. My therapy cost me thirty dollars a week and that's a pretty heavy scene. If I'd had a kid who needed new shoes or his or her teeth fixed, I'm not sure I would have been able to do it.

"How could I be so self-indulgent with a child counting on me? How could I go for long walks, or whatever it is that I do to get through these things?

"I'm thirty-four years old, and finally saying, you're OK, you're really OK. I don't know if that would have happened with kids. I might have thrown all my energy into kids so that I could forget who I was. To define myself as a parent—that's a nice convenient label. It's a handle you can grab onto. You can say, 'I'm responsible for this child.' That's wonderful, but if it gets in the way of saying you are a person, a worthwhile person, then I don't know. It's my particular self I'm talking about. Maybe other people have done it with kids, maybe with ten kids. But for me, it might have been a convenient way not to look at some things, and I might have missed learning to like myself.

"It takes a while to get to that point. I grew up with certain ways of thinking about myself—or not thinking about myself. Like leaving myself out of the picture when I thought about good people I'd like to know. Well, I want to put myself on that list of people I want to know."

I asked Steve to go back and pick up on what he had been saying about his decision being influenced by not liking himself.

"I knew I would be a good parent insofar as I could have provided the things a child would need. But I didn't have a very high estimation of myself; I felt I just couldn't hack it, I didn't have that much to give. A parent is defined as someone who has a lot to give over an extended period of time. If you don't think you have much to give, it colors your thinking about parenthood. I'm really happy to find out, though, that now that I do feel better about myself, I still feel no need to give what I have to a particular child, to have a child of my own to give it to."

Does he have any regrets?

"No, not now. Because I don't know what's going to happen

in the future. I have a lot of love to give and I give it to Anne
and to my sister, to my friends and those people I come into
contact with whom I can really open up to, and that's enough.
I want children in my life, and thank God my friends have provided them!"

Anne told her story next.

"When Steve and I were first married, I felt a sort of resentment because he didn't want children. That was a time when I
was definitely thinking I would have them. I remember thinking, boy, he's got a sister and she's young and he really relates
to her and that's why he doesn't want to have children.

"And then I thought, well, in two years we'll discuss it.
Then, as the marriage got older, and better, I thought, well, I
certainly don't need children. I was so happy the way I was, I
really didn't want them, either.

"I don't know when that decision actually came. And I look
back on my life and see the things that we would not have been
able to do if we had children. I would not have been able to
work for a period of time. Living on Steve's salary would have
been impossible. Living in a one-room, fifth floor walk-up
would have been impossible. We've traveled to Europe many
times; we've been to Mexico. I really don't see how we could
have left school in June and gone until September without a
salary. I mean, we got ourselves into debt with just the two of
us.

"With children, I just don't see how we could have bought
this place and worked on it. We'd still be back in the city. I
would not have had the time to find out who I am—I'm still
searching. I ignored a lot about myself up until about four
years ago, and if I'd had children, that's what I would have continued to do.

"We knew that if we had a child, we would give it our very
best, since it would have been our choice to have it. It doesn't
just happen, and you can't blame the child. I know that the
more love you give, the more you have to give—I was never

worried about the love we would give a child. But I was worried about the time. And the financial freedom that we have.

"I do have a profession, teaching, but I choose not to practice it, and consequently, as a woman, I'm relegated to secretarial work. It just doesn't pay well. But as little as I make, it does make it possible for us to live here. If we had children, it would be another expense. For us, it would have been a mistake. I'm glad every day of my life that we don't have children.

"I love kids, but I'm glad that I don't have the responsibility for any. I've watched other women get totally tied to their kids. Totally. To the exclusion of their husbands, to the exclusion of their social life, to the exclusion of their friends. And I could see myself slipping into that trap—breastfeeding and all that stuff. When I thought about having a child, I thought I should give everything to that child, and I'm glad that I didn't. I've never regretted it for an instant."

She spoke to Steve for a moment. "The night you told me you were going to have a vasectomy was one of the happiest nights of my life." She had to wait for the laughter to die down before she could continue. "Really, it's one of the nicest presents you can give a woman.

"Because what happened was that I had pretty well decided that I didn't want children, but loving Stephen and being married to him I was determined not to make a unilateral decision. If he had decided he wanted kids, I would have reconsidered my position. We talked about his staying home with the child and my going out to work.

"But then we came here. I had been on the pill for seven years and I went to a doctor for another prescription. He said he'd give me one for only a couple months more. He wanted me to come back with a decision, because I had been on the pill for too long. I went home and talked to Steve and told him that I was prepared to go to another doctor and lie, if necessary, about how long I'd been on the pill. That would give Steve time to think about what he wanted to do. He thought about it for a couple of months, and then told me he had made his decision to have a vasectomy.

"At that time, they were not doing the laparoscopy, and the tubal was major surgery, plus being a lot more expensive. It was a lot easier, not to mention cheaper, for Steve to have the vasectomy. I don't think it's done anything to him either emotionally or sexually."

Steve squeaked, "It changed my voice."

Then, serious, he said, "That's what brought it to a head, when Anne told me what the doc had said. That's when I knew we had to make a decision instead of just seesawing back and forth. I got in touch with a lot of feelings, and I realized that I loved the idea of having kids. All the wonderful little things you could do with children and all the wonderful things they could do with you. And how sweet it would be. But it was the idea, not the reality, of having kids that I was in love with." Anne was relieved to be off the pill. She had never liked the idea of constantly taking hormones.

"I felt so much better the first month. I wasn't nauseous in the morning. I had been for seven years, almost every morning. I'm so glad I don't have to do that any more; it's such a feeling of freedom."

If Steve had not had a vasectomy, the birth control hassle would have continued. Anne says now that she would rather risk having an abortion than use a dangerous method of birth control. But with Steve's vasectomy, neither is necessary.

Some fears of childbirth were a small part of her decision. "I have to admit to being afraid. I thought about it a lot when Steve and I were first married, because the standard then was that you went alone and had that baby. I thought about what it would be like to get in that wheelchair, to be in labor, and have to say goodbye to Stephen and go through those doors. And Lord knew what was through those doors."

Anne points to the women's movement and to the year 1969 as turning points in her decision. "I began to feel I had permission to handle my life as I wanted to handle it. It was okay, it wasn't strange, although some people still think it is strange." Some people have accused Anne and Steve of having cats as child substitutes. Steve says, "No, children are cat substitutes!" √

Anne and Steve spent seven years discussing having children. Steve remembers, "We talked about what it would be like to have kids. We thought at one time that Anne was pregnant. It was the first summer we were married. We were in Greece, on the Acropolis, talking about it, and we both got excited about it. Well, not exactly excited, but certainly not negative. We were in the first year of our marriage and these things happen, and of course that was during the time when Anne still wanted to have children."

She added, "I was not wanting to have kids right away, but I wanted kids someday. As it turned out, though, I wasn't pregnant."

A few years passed, and during that time both Anne and Steve enjoyed not having children. Anne began to think that maybe she didn't want children at all.

"The seminal book for me was *The Baby Trap* by Ellen Peck. I think it is important. She stated right at the beginning that she was not going to be fair. For some people, not having children is the happiest solution, and she presented the cases there that she had seen to be true. Basically, what she did was talk about people who had children and got screwed up by it. And it supported a lot of the things I had been thinking.

"Of course, then, there were not as many people who chose not to have children. I think I read it in 1973. I was reading it when Steve was thinking about having a vasectomy, and he read parts of it and a book on vasectomies. *Sexual Politics*, which had some very negative things to say, really scared me.

"As I get older, I realize that I am selfish. I have a lot that I need to learn to do for myself. Oh, I had that romantic fantasy about children. Babysitting gives you that romantic fantasy because you have them for a weekend and then that's it. I mean, it's delightful to play with them for a weekend, but I realize as I get older that I don't have what it takes to give that much to someone else. You have a certain responsibility towards someone you bring into your home, and I feel that responsibility very strongly. I have a lot of work to do on myself, and not having children makes that possible for me."

Steve responded, "You say that you are selfish . . . I used to use that word about myself, but now I am not comfortable with that; I prefer self-aware. When you become aware of that internal life, when you become aware of changes in yourself, I guess the summation of changes we call growth—if you take that seriously, it becomes, for me anyway, pretty consuming. Not all-consuming. I could see spending the rest of my life dealing with people who are friends, and with Anne in particular, finding out who they are and what I am.

"Am I just a biological entity? If so, then the logical thing to do is to carry on the biology. Or is there something else? Am I more than that, is there a motivating force within me? I've come full circle. I grew up a nominal Catholic, and ended up being what I would call an atheist, and now I've arrived at the point where I firmly believe I am more than this chemical mass. And to explore that, to meditate on that, is one of the primary things in my life. If you want to call that selfish, fine, but I prefer to call it self-aware.

"That is a legitimate way to live. It's not an alternative to being a parent. It's not a secondary way to live. And it is a way that I am happy with."

Anne, too, said that she had wondered if that was all there was to it, just propagating. "I don't want to propagate without wanting children. Thank God I don't have to.

"And yet I never would have missed Stephen. If children had been the price, I would have paid the price. But we've had such a wonderful life I wouldn't want to change it. If we had been living fifty years ago, I would have had to have children to have this relationship with Steve. I would have done it. But

I'm so glad it didn't turn out like that. There's not one iota of regret. I think about people in childbirth, and I think, yes, it is a wonderful experience, but not for me, not this lifetime. I have too much to learn."

Steve said, "It just depends on where you put your focus. I guess that it is possible to do both, to do deep self-exploration and be a good parent. Maybe that's one of the things we did, we set our standards too high. We can't live up to them so we won't have kids. But when you are dealing with another human being, you need to set your standards pretty high."

"I just thought of another thing," Anne commented, "that we couldn't have done with kids. This summer, we both needed some space, so we separated for two and a half months. We know a lot of people who feel that their marriages would benefit from such a separation—it certainly brought us closer together—but they have a child and it is just not feasible.

"I can only think of one marriage with children where things are working out. In fact, the kids have really helped. For everyone else I've seen, the kids have been detrimental to their relationship."

ANNE: We finally realized what we had been told wasn't true. Being an adult isn't necessarily a drag. I remember being told that when you are an adult life is not easy, life is not a bowl of cherries. I think that had some effect, at least for me. And being a parent was a lot of responsibility. Parents are people who have to say 'no' a lot of the time. Both to themselves and to their children. And we don't have to say no to anything we don't want to.

STEVE: Another thing that isn't mentioned too often is that you can have a wonderful sex life without kids. You never need to worry about being overheard or about someone needing a drink of water. And every room in the house is fair game, where with kids it's only the bedroom. Our sex life has gotten better and better.

Also, Anne and I have never had what I would call money

problems. I mean, we have never had much, but it has always been enough. We've never been on each other's case about money, and that's one of the things that people say is a big problem in marriage. Sex and money, those are the two issues people fight about a lot. Neither of those has been a problem for us.

One thing that really struck me about this couple is that they have not been subjected to a lot of pressure from their families. Anne told me, "You know, our parents go through a lot of hassles from their friends about us. People ask my mother, 'When is Anne going to have children?' I know they ask Steve's parents, too, 'When is he going to have kids, he's so good with kids, why doesn't he have a child?' But they don't pass it on to us."

STEVE: We were one time accused of being selfish. A woman told us we were selfish for not wanting children, and then the next sentence was, 'What are you going to do when you're old?' I wanted to say to her, 'Isn't that a selfish reason to want children, worrying about your old age?' There definitely are selfish reasons for wanting children.

Steve and Anne have chosen a hard road for themselves. They are exploring the path of finding out what it is to be human with neither a role as parents nor set careers for defining that path. Their relationship must be sustained by qualities totally unrelated to obligations to children or financial necessity. They have decided that traditional roles, either as breadwinners in secure professions or as parents, are not right for them today. Tomorrow will have to take care of itself. Somehow, I trust that it will do just that.

I left knowing they had made the best choice, but still feeling, irrationally, a little sad; they have so much love and intelligence to give. But, as they said, they can contribute those things in many other ways than by having children of their own. Perhaps they are even freer to do so because they have no children.

5

Jessica and Richard

Expanding the Meaning of Reproduction

I FIRST TALKED with Jessica and Richard at their house on a gloriously warm day in May. Jessica had told me to come prepared to walk up to the house, because the road to their hill was still in bad shape from the ravages of winter and spring.

After a nice uphill walk, I came to the base of another hill, this one with a large house perched at the top and a tiny cabin at the base. According to the instructions I'd been given, this was it. I climbed the hill.

Going around to the door, I knocked and was greeted by Jessica, who laughingly explained, "We're early risers, but we're also late starters." At 10:30 on a Sunday morning, they were lingering over a last cup of coffee before going down to lay out a huge garden for the five people who would come to help plant it the following weekend.

I had a tour of their magnificent house—built by their own hands—and then we all trooped down to the garden. We all busied ourselves putting in stakes, labeling them for about twenty different vegetables, and stretching string between the stakes to mark the area to be planted with each vegetable.

It wasn't until we had done a lot of talking about things in general, and had a bit of wine and cheese down by the stream,

45

that we began the interview itself. I took notes while we talked; they put in the onion sets.

For this couple, the decision not to have children was primarily a political and social one. Jessica and Richard are intelligent, articulate people who talked about many of the political and social issues they considered before deciding to stay childfree.

Both Jessica and Richard had difficult family lives. How much that affected their decision not to have children is unclear; I have no intention of trying to analyze that influence. I don't think they had unraveled it for themselves at the time I talked with them. Childhood pain can linger in our lives, affecting us in ways that we only slowly, if ever, recognize.

Jessica grew up in a city in the Midwest. Her neighborhood had lots of kids, and people got along well together. Her family was constantly anxious about money, but they lived in a nice, modest house, and her parents somehow provided money for riding and music lessons. But the three children felt that they paid with guilt for what they had.

Jessica also thinks that she was an emotionally abused child. Deeply buried memories have come out in therapy, and one of her two brothers has confirmed memories of a mother who harangued the children mercilessly, raved, screamed, and was at times incoherent. Her father, the victim of a childhood marked by humiliation, tended to be very hard on his own children.

Her childhood was colored by "an overwhelming sense of tragedy." The message from her Jewish family was, "You can only trust your own family and other Jews." It felt like a trap.

When Jessica told her mother that she had had her tubes tied, her mother said, "How could you mutilate yourself that way?" Her father met the news with "sullen silence." But she is still the child they have the most positive contact with.

Richard's family was not abusive, but the circumstances at home were difficult. His mother had Hodgkin's disease and lived for many years in great pain, unable to take care of the household. His parents had a good relationship, however, and everyone in the family worked together to get things done and take care of his mother. Richard grew up doing housework and also learned the electrician's trade from his father. At seventeen, he joined the army. Both of Richard's parents are dead now.

Jessica had thought little about having kids until she and Richard started going together. It had not been an assumption in her life. They met in college, married, followed many of the traditional paths. They are now both in their thirties; Richard is five years older than Jessica. Both have been surgically sterilized. Richard had a vasectomy about six years ago, but they had decided several years before that not to have children. Jessica had a laparoscopy several years after Richard's vasectomy because she was still having trouble with the decision—for her there was still the possibility of having children. At that time, too, monogamy was an issue they were discussing. "I would have kept rethinking this," Jessica told me, "as I do everything, if I had not had that operation."

JESSICA: I have been thinking about continuity—about people needing to feel that something isn't going to end, like a family isn't going to end. I feel fairly certain that the dismay my parents expressed was around that issue—seeing something end. And certainly it's something I had to deal with in making my decision: realizing, admitting the reality of things ending, of families ending, of life ending. There is a basic assumption that the longevity of something is part of its worth.

The whole issue of worth and things lasting is molded into our culture. It was something I had to grapple with. It was much more difficult for me to accept that, as a species, we are coming to an end on this planet, than it was to accept that my family line was coming to an end. I've had to come to terms with the environment's demise. As you can tell, I'm no optimist.

Jessica describes a time when she was proselytizing anybody who would listen to her. "I was taking very personally every person who went ahead and had a kid; we are overrun with human population, to the devastation of our species and the landscape—we live heavily on the land.

"But it can get to you if you think about it too much. The defense we use is to think about it less, and go on living. I plan to live my life without going bonkers." She feels better if she lives her life in ways that don't contribute too much to an already bad situation. "So I don't eat meat and I don't have children and I try not to burn too much oil."

"After Richard had the vasectomy, he ended the whole issue, for himself. I wasn't included in that, not because of anything he said or did, but because I had not come to a decision about it. I tend to mull things over, and I didn't want to mull this over any more. I wanted to go on to other things, use my energy for other things. Which brings me to energy.

"Spending my energy raising a child would, I think, be very disappointing for me—looking back every two to three years, realizing that this is how I'm spending my time. People describe me as terribly energetic, but my energy is intense and in short spurts. And I need lots of peace and quiet to build it up again. That's not the kind of thing having children is compatible with.

"I thought a lot about my lifestyle and what my life would look like and what it would sound like when I was making my decision. I like a lot of quiet and being able to hear the wind in the trees and the birds without constantly being interrupted by someone else rapping at me. So I'm pleased about that. My life feels good."

I asked Richard how their decision evolved, since they had both mentioned earlier that they "sort of" thought they would have children when they decided to marry. Richard corrected me. "Well, let's say that I was more accepting then of the stereotype of what getting married meant. My sureness that we would have children was just evidence that I had never worked the stereotype through. I had never questioned it. As my view of that world crumbled, so did that expectation. The changes were caused by thinking about things I once took for granted. But it didn't follow automatically that I stopped thinking about having children. It was really when people began taking us aside and saying, 'Gee, we noticed you don't have children yet, don't blow it by having them.' (laughs) And that caused us to reflect on why there are so many unhappy parents. Some of those people also told us that after having children, their love was never the same. It shook us up.

"I think that is all it took, for someone to say, 'Hey, it might not be an incredibly good thing for you to become someone's parents.' And then there were professional reasons for delaying the decision, and after that, there was a whole host of reasons, political, ecological, social, personal, in terms of expenditure of our time and money. So it happened by stages. And since we made the decision not to become parents, I haven't really had any second thoughts about it."

During the interview, I began to feel a little uneasy that our whole conversation was going to be on a very intellectual level. I expressed that to Richard and Jessica, and Jessica said that she did not want it to be a purely intellectual interview. All of the important and heavy decisions in her life had a gut level element. But she also felt strongly that she did not want people to read this and say, 'Oh, yeah, they just didn't want to give up that money or that boat, whatever,' and think that the intellectual element was so much rationalizing. "Maybe that is why I downplay the gut level part."

"I'm not dedicated to the persistence of the human species. In fact, I'd rate us pretty low among those who should go out and live on the earth. I can't tell you my phenomenal disappointment in human beings. And I own part of that, too.

"I've heard people blithely condemn people who don't have children as people who have written off the human race. I'm not prepared to argue that isn't correct. Maybe I have. But maybe that's not bad."

I said that it would be possible to argue the other side just as strongly—that those who are breeding unconsciously are writing off the human race by their actions.

"I feel that I'm behaving as if I haven't written it off, while many other people seem to have a 'me first' attitude. They live in their own little world," she said.

"The children in this neighborhood come from very different backgrounds from either of us, and we are the only adults in this area who will talk to them. They come trotting up here on their horses and we don't run them off or tell them to go away. We listen to them. It took them a while, I think, to get over the idea that we weren't overgrown kids. It's mind-expanding for them, and I know it is for me.

"There was a couple who lived on our block when I was a little girl, and my parents would always warn us to stay away from their house because they didn't have any children and didn't like children. Later I found out the husband was a pediatrician.

"I think some parents direct a certain amount of hostility at people who don't have children. I wouldn't be surprised if some of that hasn't been directed at us. But the children still come up to visit."

RICHARD: I would like to argue against the relevance of the gut level. It seems to me that the likely contents of our gut level sensibilities are going to be cultural and environmental, as opposed to reflective and critical. It seems to me that unless feelings can stand the scrutiny of an extra-socialized perspective, they should be suspect. Certainly they are not a starting point or an ending point for action.

JESSICA: On a gut level, I appreciate the type of life and the type of relationship we're able to live. We're very much in control of our time. And for two such serious political heavies, we have a lot more fun than most of the folks who live around here. Every time we see these people, we are struck by the lack of laughter and fun in their lives.

For us, doing the work, whether it is harvesting firewood or putting up siding, or whatever, is fun. And on days that we don't feel good working, or just don't feel good, we can sit down and take that feeling apart, we can talk. We do the work because we have decided to do it. We don't have too much choice about other aspects of our lives. But here we have lots of choices. We can take physical risks and emotional risks.

RICHARD: It certainly is the case for many people that the decision to be parents is a decision to opt for a non-risk-taking cover under which they can slide their own anxieties and turn them into obligations to their children.

One of the common features of faculty members that I ran into when I was trying to prevent the political firing of several colleagues, was that they routinely used the fact of having children as the reason they had to be careful about losing their jobs. They would not take a public stance. They might contribute a few dollars if no one would know they had done it. I think that is their own timidity, and having children simply confers on it a legitimacy it might otherwise lack. It's an excuse for taking the easiest course.

JESSICA: If I decide not to go to a demonstration against nuclear power, I have to own that reason myself. I don't have an excuse. It's not that my kids will be shipped off to become wards of the state if I get busted.

"You said that children give people a good, easy way to escape risks?" I asked.

RICHARD: Yes, socially unrewarded risks. If you take on some socially reinforced risks, such as good parenting, they are the ones everyone takes on. Praise is automatic and I think not very sincere. And blameworthiness is directed at people who do it badly. You are supposed to be a parent, and if you blow it, you're culpable. And not being a parent is seen as a threatening way out for a lot of people who are parents or are going to be. I don't think everyone who is a parent is threatened by non-parents, but I think it is true of enough people to be a particular social problem—the notion of having to be someone else's provider and therefore having one's options curtailed.

JESSICA: I know people who won't even subscribe to a socialist magazine, because if it got out in town their kids would have to take a lot of shit at school. Children are made to carry the burden of their parents' bad faith. Sure, people worry about losing their jobs. But I'm talking about children being made almost scapegoats: if it weren't for you, I could have written that book, made that speech, taken that stand. I feel people hide behind their children's skirts, in some cases. When I'm optimistic I think that. When I'm pessimistic, I think most people don't have those stands to take anyhow.

RICHARD: It's not the ones who are oblivious who bother me. It's the ones who are being careful. They don't have a crisis of conscience about their colleagues who are in dire straits. Informed citizens, who are in a position to know what their responsibilities are and who should be able to see the politics of a situation often will admit that action is necessary, but they say they can't do anything. They disqualify themselves from doing anything because they have their kids to take care of. The bad faith of being careful and safe careerists is passed off onto their children.

Jessica and Richard are not necessarily saying that they could or would do any better. They are simply saying that they have chosen not to get into a situation which would very likely encourage them to act the same way.

JESSICA: I think not having children or something else as an excuse forces me to come to terms with myself, to know where my energy stops or where my commitments don't overcome my fears.

RICHARD: Jessica is, I think, much more pessimistic about the future of things ecologically than I am. She has often pointed out that we have passed the ecological point of no return. My view assumes that we haven't. There is still time to do something, if we are careful about what we consume, and live accordingly. Strategies have to be predicated on what you'd lose the most by if you are wrong. It seems that both of us have sufficient expectations of the future to live as we do.

We built a house that can last a couple of hundred years. And we're trying to establish for ourselves a style of life that we suppose will be a tenable style of life for the future. We hope that this place will offer people with similar inclinations a way of life that won't be an ecological disaster. But I think both of us are highly doubtful about there being a sufficient number of us, at least at this juncture in history, to turn things around quickly.

My job gives me a place where I can get paid for a few hours a week to talk to people about all of this. So there is a place where I can invest some energy in the futures of other people. I guess we both believe in enough of a chance of a future not to render futile the sorts of things we are doing.

JESSICA: I remember sitting down at one point in my life and thinking about what it would be like to not have had kids and be seventy. I pictured myself there, and thought about what the day-to-day thing would feel like, even though I wasn't as aware then of the day-to-day process being even more important than the goal. Obviously, I decided that I wouldn't mind being that old lady. And I thought about having friends who were also in their seventies, maybe some younger. Having kids is no assurance that you won't be alone when you are old.

This "when you are old" theme kept coming up. Sometimes I wonder if having children doesn't work against having deep friendships with peers since people tend to spend their developmental years as adults taking care of children. I expressed this thought to Richard and Jessica, and she told me, "I was talking with my mother—who recently was diagnosed as having skin cancer, although it looks as if everything is going to be okay—and she talked about all the stress in her life. She said it was good to talk to me, because she didn't really have anyone to talk to. I asked about her friends, and she said, 'I wouldn't want to burden them.' My God, if I couldn't go to my friends with heavy stuff, I wouldn't consider them friends. Maybe if you have children you tend to get walled off from making close friendships that can take that kind of burden."

RICHARD: It seems to me the whole notion of the family is in dramatic need of rethinking, at a time when there are four and a half billion people on the earth. It is time to go back to scratch and ask, which of the institutions are still viable and which aren't? Which constitute making virtues of necessities which are no longer necessities? When there was no way to alter patterns of conception, there was a tendency to make a virtue of what might not really have been all that interesting or desirable.

Clearly this is the time for thinking out alternatives to social institutions which no longer function. We can certainly afford to have significant numbers of us not reproducing at all. There might even be good arguments for as many of us who can forgo it to do so, since the question of how much of the earth there is to divide among however many of us there are, is surely going to be a central question in the future of humankind.

It seems to me that we need to reverse the present cultural situation in which you have children unless you can think of some reason not to. It should change to a situation in which you don't have children unless you can think of some good reasons *to*. This would change the patterns that lead to unwanted children, to child abuse, to unreflective shoving of everyone towards first the altar and then the maternity ward. There are no really compelling personal reasons for me to have children, and there are lots of sound social reasons not to.

JESSICA: And that brings me down to a real dilemma. What is the most precious thing you share with someone you love in this culture? It's having children. And if you don't have children together, it's not really love. What substitute is there that is recognized not only by the two people in love, but by everyone else? How do you show that you are sharing something precious? What can people do to manifest their love?

We have friends who had a baby about the same time we started getting into this homestead, and she remarked one time, "We had a kid and you had a house." It seems that people are searching for some symbol, because the relationship itself is too ethereal. This house is just a by-product of a process of growth and change we went through together. But a kid is something everyone can marvel at. And there is such a hype about having a kid.

RICHARD: It seems to me that the reasons why people usually have children are the same reasons why they are less than apt parents. The psychologically most compelling reasons are often the most disqualifying reasons—needing to live on through someone else. That almost always means fulfilling one of your own dreams through someone else, a sure formula for the tyrannical parent and the misbehaving child.

JESSICA: I think it is immature of people to think that they have to have every experience in life. We must come to terms with the fact that there is a lot we are not going to do. I remember a woman who used to be at Zero Population Growth, and she was a very confirmed nonparent. Then she got married and right away wanted to have a kid. She said she didn't want to miss out on having that experience. What she may not have been seeing was that by having that experience, she was missing other ones. I'm not saying that she should have chosen not to be a parent, but we are fooling ourselves if we think we are not passing up anything.

There is something almost pioneering about people who are not having children and are very clear about their reasons.

RICHARD: Plus I think there is a real distinction between reasons that take account of everyone's individual behavior within the social context and those which benefit just the individual. I gather from what you have said and from almost everyone I've talked to over the years that in thinking about not being a parent, the overwhelming reasons are almost always the latter. That is seen as the appropriate light in which you discuss the issue. Whether there might also be some social questions which might be affected by how you make the decision never arises.

That doesn't mean that we haven't gained some personal and financial benefits from not being parents. But that isn't what made it possible for me to decide that I would never regret it. I couldn't get to the point of having the vasectomy, of burning that bridge, until I was sure that there was no reason I should ever regret it. There was no way I could have done that on 'me' reasons alone. There would have been no way for me to know that 'me' wouldn't want something else later.

I can't forsee a scenario within the next ten or twenty years which would be likely to change the nature of my social obligations as I now understand them. If tomorrow the population really drastically reduced and the goods of the world were more equitably distributed, if a whole host of needed social changes were accomplished, it would still not be clear that I would need to be someone's parent. There would still be a lot of other important and satisfying things to do. But in this way I have resolved questions about what I might feel in the future. Otherwise, I might get into a kind of response for which there is no good reason, which comes out of a loaded cultural context.

I can remember when Jessica and I were going through some early and some fundamental questions around roles, male and female. I was standing there doing the dishes—I had done household duties as a child, so it wasn't all that strange—but I remember thinking that I knew what the old role was. That was all clear and laid out, I knew where it was all going. And I had a flash of anxiety. I was unclear about what the future of my life was going to look like. If the expectations that I had in the past were now connected to a role that I saw as undesirable, what was to replace them? I think it was a general fear of the unknown.

I think we need lots of people around who have the freedom to think about what life is for besides reproducing and find some creative answers to that question. They also need to start acting on their thinking, start restructuring our institutions, so that there is no longer the automatic expectation of biological reproduction.

We need to expand our notion of reproduction so that we can start talking about human interaction as a way of reproducing—ways of being in the world, styles of life, modes of relating to each other. We need to see the structure of the community, the culture, the society, as a significant reproductive act by itself. It's clear we affect the future. If many of us were not locked into the nuclear family and the breadwinning role, but were involved with friends of all ages in a wide variety of contexts we could shape the culture a lot more than by nurturing just one child.

It's kind of an isolated model, the parent-child relationship. To deny the label of significant reproductive activity to all those social activities which are seen now as peripheral to parenting is a pronatalist notion of reproduction.

Jessica gets really turned off by people who say to her, "You really ought to have a kid—I just had one and it's wonderful." She and Richard call this the "consumer theory of decision-making."

RICHARD: It's okay to jump the track if you allow it to be explained as an idiosyncrasy. If it is just a personal, subjective thing, you are a little eccentric, but it is all right. But if you suggest that there are good reasons why you jumped the track and that those reasons apply to large numbers of people who haven't yet jumped, they get very uneasy and their supposition is that there is something to be defended.

Jessica returned for a moment to how she feels when people see her with children or in the classes she teaches and tell her what a wonderful parent she would make. "It's as if, if you have that kind of nurturing potential, if you have originality, spark, fun, you better put it into childraising, because there is nothing else in our society which cuts the mustard."

Richard adds, "For a woman I think that is just raging sexism, thinly disguised, that all female nurturance has to go into parenthood."

"Many philosophers say that the essence of being human is being a free, creative, producing animal. That is not how most people are living. People have been oppressed by being told that their jobs depend on acceptance of things like nuclear power, rampant consumerism, a waste economy, and I see that as going back to the whole need to be the family breadwinner for one or more children whose existence may or may not have been a thoughtful choice."

Many of us feel distressed by the knowledge that those who already see the crisis of dwindling resources don't need to be convinced and those who don't see it may be impossible to convince. We don't like to think that a major crisis would be the only thing that could do the convincing. Richard says that he thinks a gradual deterioration of the quality of life will do more than a major crisis, because it will affect almost everyone. But we won't get the choice of tactics.

Our talk drifted to the question of ultimate purpose of human life. It is possible, we agreed, that we are here to enjoy, in the fullest sense of the word. But we would like to do that in a way that replenishes the earth as well as takes from it.

Richard went back and commented on something I had said earlier about feeling nurturant toward the whole human race. "I am afraid that parenthood often dampens that feeling. I see a predisposition in parents to have a stake in a certain portion of the human race, and that specific stake often makes them act in ways that cut off the possibilities for the rest of humankind.

Unfortunately, in our world making things better for your kid may involve making things worse for other people's kids."

Because Jessica and Richard don't have children, they have often been able to help other people. They have given them money, a place to live, a transition place. "Our charity is purely political, and it is no sacrifice because we don't need the money anyway, partly because we don't regard a lot of things as needs."

Jessica summed things up for herself. "Making plans based on my ideas and beliefs and then living out those plans is really important to me. And not having children is an example of that."

Richard, I guess, didn't want us to end on a serious note, after all the heavy political and social stuff we'd just been through. "Yes," he said, "it has taken us years to work out all these after-the-fact justifications!"

6

Greg and Susan

A Realization, Not a Decision

I DROVE DOWN to a small college town to meet Greg and Susan on a warm day in January. The sky was overcast, but the clouds occasionally lifted to reveal long gray and white views of the hills and valleys.

I arrived a little early, so when no one answered my knock, I waited in my car. The house, in an old section of town, looked well-kept, modest. I didn't know much about this couple except that Greg taught at the college. They had called in response to one of the posters I had put up.

When Susan drove up, she looked very outdoorsy. She seemed very confident as well. We went in, greeted the dog, and I looked around while Susan started making tea. The furniture was mostly, if not all, antiques; the rooms were neat, cheerful, and inviting.

Both Susan and Greg are college graduates, and both grew up in small towns. Neither has a strong ethnic background. Susan's family was very religious; Greg's was not. Now, religion is not a significant part of their lives. They are in their middle thirties and have been married for ten years.

In sharp contrast to the difficult childhoods described in the last interview, Greg and Susan both tell of happy, peaceful

60

families. Their parents are alive, and family relationships are warm, affectionate, respectful.

After Greg arrived home from work, we all settled down with cups of tea. I asked how they came to a decision not to have children. Greg began by saying, "I don't remember ever making a decision. At various times I would say, 'I don't want to have any children *now*,' but I wasn't asking, 'Do I *ever* want to have children?' As time went by, though, I didn't feel more like I wanted to have children. Somewhere, I began to realize that it was getting kind of late, but I still felt I didn't want to have children now, and that probably meant never. We didn't ever say we had decided not to have children. It was more of a realization."

Susan and Greg were twenty-four when they married. Susan said that although they talked about many other things before deciding to marry, they did not discuss whether to have children. Greg disagrees. He remembers that they both said they did not want to have children right away.

They talked about it later, after years of marriage. Susan told me, "I think we both felt lucky that the other person felt the same way." According to Greg, they both "just eventually realized that it seemed unlikely they would have children."

Susan said, "In my own mind, two or three years ago, I felt pretty strongly that I didn't want to have children."

I asked Greg, "You said that you kept saying you were not going to have kids *yet*. Did that mean you were assuming that you would have children?"

"I don't think there was that assumption. It was just a matter of not thinking down the line very far. We were resolving for now that we were not going to have kids. But we were not deciding that we either were or were not going to. I know the way I felt then was that I didn't want to have children then, and although I couldn't imagine ever wanting children, most people do. We thought maybe we would change our minds, but it just never happened."

Susan's older sister began having children at the age of eighteen; Susan feels that this influenced her decision. She knew for certain that she did not want to have children when she was young. "I realized the impact of children on people's lives." Susan helped take care of her sister's children, and realized that having children at that age meant missing a free and fun young adulthood. "It was quite powerful." She enjoyed taking care of the children, but says, "I had friends who enjoyed it more. I never have been one to just run to babies, but I am attracted to them a little—I don't run *away*, either. I did baby-sit and I enjoyed it, and I sat with my nieces and nephews, and loved that. But I always knew what an impact they were on my sister's life and the lives of my friends. Although I had no thoughts of never having children, I had no thoughts of having them, either."

Many couples delay having children until one or both of them are through college and graduate school. I asked Greg if graduate school was one of the reasons they put off the question of having children. He replied, "That was the first excuse."

He had several more years of school, they had no money, and Susan was working. "But," she says, "I didn't have at the back of my mind that when Greg finished school, then . . ."

Having children has never been much of a part of either Greg's or Susan's thinking. Greg never felt that he wanted children and could not forsee a time when he would. I asked him if he could think of anything that might have influenced him, but he could not think of anything in the past that might have turned him off the idea of having children. It seemed that things in the present were the more important influences.

"The main factor for me was that we like to travel and do a lot of things. We didn't want to be prevented from doing those things, for a few years, anyway. We wanted to be free to do what we wanted before we were tied down to kids. We still feel that way, I guess; we are fairly active and we still like to travel.

On weekends there is always a lot of backpacking or canoeing or hiking or skiing."

Their friends with similar interests have all had children. I asked if that had made a noticeable difference in the active lives of those friends. The answer was, "Definitely."

"We are aware that when we say 'Let's do this or that,' it is always difficult for them to be able to do it with us. They couldn't be gone for very long or they couldn't go at all, or else they had to bring the kids, and that causes problems. Money is always a problem. Hiring a sitter, even for an event that is free, costs a lot. You never, never, do anything on the spur of the moment. I love to call up somebody at twenty of five and invite them over for spaghetti and then go out skiing afterward. But you have to plan and book ahead to do something if you have a child."

Greg added, "Susan just mentioned money. That is a part of liking to travel and do things. All those things take money, and we didn't feel we would be able to afford to do as much of it. What do they say the average cost of a child is from birth to age twenty? Something like $70,000, I think?"

SUSAN: I think I knew that there would be something missing if we didn't raise children. There is something very special about children. And I have a very special feeling about my parents and very fond memories of my childhood. It was very happy.

Greg's childhood was happy , too. "But it is not clear to me how happy my childhood was for my parents, which is really what we are talking about. We could provide a happy childhood for our kids, but how happy would it be for us?"

SUSAN: I remember someone saying to me a few years ago, "It is a shame you don't have children, because you are so bright and so great and so loving, you would be such a good parent." And I said there is no question that I could be a good parent. I feel eminently qualified to be a good parent. But it would be at a cost. I'm sure it would be a pleasurable relationship and a loving relationship, something very special, but I really don't want to do that.

Having children would probably change our relationship. I feel that it is very different from my friends' relationships, and I think part of that is that we have more time and energy for each other. I also feel that our marriage is permanent, but it could change. As a woman, I would not want to be alone with the responsibility of children. It would be very confining. I don't feel marriage as confining.

How have their families approached the question of children?

GREG: It must be clear by now to my parents that we are not going to have children. My mother has never said anything at all. My father has never said anything directly about it, but occasionally he's made some comments that lead me to believe that maybe if he had it to do all over again, he would be less inclined to have kids. Or not as many. I remember one time, not long after Susan and I were married, when my sister needed someone to stay overnight with her kids, and my father said, "Well, maybe you should do it, so you can get an idea about whether you want to get into that or not."

Once Susan decided to talk to Greg's mother, so that she would know there was no problem. Susan knew that her mother-in-law would never ask, because she has made a real point of staying out of things that are between Susan and Greg. Susan told her that they did not know if they would ever have children, but that so far they had not wanted them.

Susan talked about her family. "My father feels children are very special, he loves them, loves his grandchildren. I feel that because my sister had children, she helped me out a lot. My father had such a wonderful time with his daughters that I'm sure it is hard for him to imagine why I would not want that. I think my mother would understand more, but we haven't discussed it. What she wouldn't understand was why I didn't want to do my duty. She is a duty person—do your fair share in life. I'm pretty sure that in some ways she feels disappointed. I feel kind of bad, too—it must be nice to have grandchildren."

This couple has decided that Greg should have a vasectomy. The decision followed an accidental pregnancy which necessitated an abortion. This was their first pregnancy, and although having the abortion was not a difficult decision for them, it certainly was not a pleasant thing to have to do. Susan felt nothing but relief when it was over. None of the available birth control methods, short of sterilization, are completely safe and effective. All of them are a hassle. A vasectomy simplifies life a great deal.

I asked Susan if she felt a sense of loss about missing the experience of being a parent. "I feel that my life would be different—I am giving up something. But I can't describe it as a loss. I don't think in thirty years I will wish I had a kid. I don't think I will feel lonely in my old years. You know, one of the women who had the most to say to me about having a child was an older woman in the South who hadn't left there her whole life. She was a poor woman who had children and had a wonderful time with them. She wasn't a close friend, but she felt she could tell me that I should have children. She used to tell me that I will be lonely in my old age. But I know you can't rely on children to provide friendships when you are old. I will miss a very close relationship that I would have with a child, but it is not like I'm depriving myself of something, not a terrible loss.

"I know that I will have friends. That will go on. I also know that I will be able to take care of myself. I will not need children for that. I am not sure I would want them to, anyway."

Susan showed me a wonderful picture of four generations of women in her family. We marveled at the cumbersome, ornate-looking clothes. Once in a while, Susan says, she thinks about what it means for her to end the family line. This is a hard question for many people. Do they have the right to end the genetic family line? And what about the style, the tone, of your

particular family? It took so long to get to you. For many people, this question would have been the hardest one, if their
brothers and sisters, like Susan's, hadn't helped them out by
having children.

Any regrets? "Oh no. I feel that we are making this decision,
that we have talked about it. It is important to us, the things
we are getting in exchange for what we are giving up."

Susan is presently working at a job that requires her to be
away from home four days a week. She works with mildly retarded adults. I commented that it would be difficult for her to
do that if she had a child. She agreed, but was quick to point
out that she does not have to be doing something that keeps
her moving back and forth like that. She likes the job and is
glad for the opportunity and the freedom to do it.

"When I applied for the job, the man who was in charge
said, 'Why do you want this job?' He viewed it as having children to care for. But it isn't. The people I work with are adults.
Retarded people aren't like children. They sometimes do
things that are a little childlike, but not childish. And it is
definitely not like they were my children. I can leave after four
days."

Susan and Greg have noticed no particular response to their
not having children. Most of their friends don't seem to give it
a thought, even though they have children.

"We have known only one couple who were friends who did
not have children, but that was a couple where one wanted a
child and the other didn't. We knew another couple here for
several years before they had a child, but now they have one.
We have noticed what has happened to them.

"Right up until the child was born, the husband, especially,
was going around saying how this was not going to change anything. His wife was going to take a leave and then was going to
go back to work in a couple of months. They have always
skiied with us, and they were going to keep doing that, nothing
was going to change. It has been almost a year now, and she is

still not back at work and they no longer go out and do things like they used to."

I have heard this story before. Anyone who thinks nothing will change is not facing the reality of having another person to consider, especially a little person who needs a lot of your time and energy and attention. To choose to have a child is to choose change. I'm not saying that you must give everything to your child. But neither can you expect things to go on just as they did before.

We all agreed that it helps a lot if you have family in the same town, so that you have a few willing and able babysitters close at hand. But find out beforehand if your family wants to do it. Assumptions can be dangerous.

What about the question of selfishness? Greg answered. "We have heard that occasionally. I think the woman that Susan mentioned before sort of implied that it was selfish. In a way, it *is* selfish, because we are saying that we want more time and more money to do the things we want to do. I guess I don't necessarily think being selfish is bad. And it leaves more time and money for other people as well, not just yourself. You can do things in the community.

"I think the way the word selfish is usually used implies another person, so I don't think it really applies here. If the child already existed and you were ignoring it because you wanted the time and money, that would be selfish. But we are talking about a person who doesn't exist. Having children around deprives you in so many ways that maybe it helps people to feel that they are being selfless or giving something in a noble way. It makes it easier."

I asked if there were any larger social issues involved in their choice not to have children. Greg said, "Population and other issues have always been in my mind. I was always sure that I would not want to have more than one or two kids, and it makes me feel good, in a way, that I don't have children. If I thought I wanted to have kids, I would have a conflict with that. But I don't think it has been important in coming to this point."

SUSAN: I feel strongly that somewhere down the line, probably within our lifetime, population is going to become a terrible, terrible problem. I feel good that I am not contributing to that. I also wonder what it would be like for a child I would have. I know the quality of life is going to be so different. I fear that it might not be healthful and good. But that wasn't a major reason.

I asked Greg and Susan if they could think of anything they could not do if they had children. They said it is not really a matter of anything being impossible. But money would be tighter, and simply because of the logistics they would probably do fewer of the things they now enjoy. Some of their friends have expressed envy about the spontaneous way they can decide to go out for an evening or away for a weekend.

SUSAN: I also think it is important for us to have things quiet. I don't imagine too many people have mentioned that.

GREG: Maybe you get used to it, I don't know. But I know every time we have friends over, especially one who brings two small children, it's fun, but I'm really tired at the end of it. Mostly I'm just tired of the noise and confusion.

I asked Greg if he felt, as Susan does, that he would be a good parent. He said it is a little hard for him to figure out what being a good parent really means, and that even if you are a good parent, you don't have any guarantees that the kid will turn out okay. But aside from that, he is not sure about his capabilities as a parent. He wonders if he could put up with the noise, the frustration. But when he looks around at other people who are parents, he thinks, "It seems to me I would be as good as most of them." Still, he's not sure.

I said that the lack of relief from parenthood is what scares me the most—there is nothing in my life I have not needed relief from.

GREG: When we go to visit friends with children, I can see

how often I would be very exasperated if I were responsible for them for long periods of time. It is really hard for me to accept how unreasonable they are. When they start screaming and hollering about something that is totally unreasonable, I just don't know how I would put up with that.

It has come up several times today, the idea that there is some sort of loss in not having children. I guess I have to say that I don't feel that way. There is a possibility I will feel later on that I am missing something, but right now, I am not convinced that I am losing anything. But even if I do come to think that it would have been better for me to have had children, both decisions are irreversible. And it is equally likely that there are losses in having children.

SUSAN: Someone said to me, "Well, why don't you have just one child?" But there is a world of difference between none and one. That's where the real change is. It doesn't come after two or three.

Do they know anyone who regrets having children? Susan does. "I have a friend who said, 'They are people now, and I love them, but if I had it to do over, I would not.' The relationship with the kids is fine. But she can say that she goofed. She also didn't like the way it changed her relationship with her spouse."

GREG: The "experience of being a parent." These words don't have much meaning for me. I can't understand any part of it. I mean, it is an experience, obviously, but the implication is that it is something that is good, that no one should miss. But I just can't think about any part of it that I am unhappy not to have.

SUSAN: (laughs) I would say there is not much ambivalence here!

I have a friend who has a child under a year old, and she is having a really difficult time. I told her that I was trying to feel for her, but that I was having a hard time doing that, because I know she made the decision to have the child. In the old days, you just had them, but now you decide. And it is really hard for me to understand why people do, at least why so many do. It surprises me, now that things are changing, for women especially, that so many of them are having children rather than taking the option not to. Most of my friends have children."

I told them that many people still do not see it as an option. There are still strong expectations that people have children.

GREG: Yes, it is promoted in lots of subtle ways. When people on TV quiz shows are asked how many children they have and they say eight, the audience applauds.

Most of Susan's friends got married and had children, except for one woman who is probably her best friend. But Susan went to college, which delayed things a bit. "Well," she said, "at least you have an excuse; you are doing something worthwhile." It struck me that she used the word excuse. Do we need to have an excuse for not having children? Yes, I guess at times it has seemed that way.

Probably the greatest influence on Susan, though, was the talks she had with her parents. They told her, "It is fine to marry, fine to have children, but you don't have to do that right away, you know. It would be fine to wait until you are thirty to get married." Sage advice.

"I remember my dear, dear father saying, 'You are a gorgeous, attractive woman, and everyone is going to want to marry you.' Which is not true, but he said it. He told me I would have no problem marrying, I could choose from a lot of people, I could wait and choose someone very special.

"I am very grateful for that message. I never felt that I had to marry soon or a certain kind of person. I remember talking with my father when I was seriously thinking of marrying Greg. I was trying to convince Dad how great Greg was, and I told Dad what he was doing. Dad said, 'That's fine, but I want to know something. Does he really care about you and is he a loving, sensitive person?' I'll never forget that.

"Many of my friends had children pretty young, but I had a lot of support from my parents not to do that, which was much more important for me. They are people who do not tell me what to do; they have always told their children that their decisions will be just right. Make them yourself, you can do it. They may tell me what their thinking is, but the decision has always been mine."

After I turned off the tape recorder, Susan said that she still wonders a little why she does not have the urge to have children. She feels a little abnormal at times. "I feel like something may be missing in my make-up."

Then, as we all stood in the doorway to say goodbye, the subject of grandchildren came up again. I said that I could understand why people want grandchildren. There could be a feeling of "I earned grandchildren by having children." And people probably desire children in their lives that they are not responsible for all the time.

Susan wanted to read my book and asked me to let her know when it came out. "Sometimes it is very lonely to be the only couple without children."

7

Helen and Scott Nearing

The Good Life without Children

GOING TO VISIT HELEN AND SCOTT NEARING was, for me, something like making a pilgrimage. From 1932 to 1952, the Nearings lived in the backwoods of Vermont, growing their own food, sugaring, building stone houses, depending on the outside world for very little. I had read their book, *Living the Good Life*, subtitled *How to Live Sanely and Simply in a Troubled World*, describing why and how they did it.

When I read that book, five years ago, I felt that I had indeed found some sanity and simplicity in an often crazy and needlessly complex world. The life they described was whole, frugal, simple, and healthful. It took and gave back harmoniously with the natural world. And it was disciplined in a way that I admired. Each member of the household worked four hours a day at "bread labor," growing food, cutting wood, building shelter, doing survival tasks. Each person also had four hours a day to devote to avocation—writing, painting, music, reading, thinking, whatever that person did in response to creative urges. Finally, each person had four hours to spend with other people. An enviable schedule, to my mind. This is a life in which you create your own luxuries rather than buy them—and one of the greatest luxuries is time. You buy time by needing less of everything else.

72

The Nearings now live in Maine, doing many of the same things there which worked so well for them in Vermont. As of this writing, Scott is ninety-six. Helen is seventy-five. They have been together for over forty years. I was delighted when, in response to my letter requesting an interview, I got Helen's note inviting me for lunch, "noonish," on a certain Saturday.

Helen was out in the yard when I drove in, and from the way she looked at me, I felt warmly welcomed even before she spoke a word. As I walked toward the magnificent stone house they had recently completed, she began telling me that her mother was Dutch. She leaned the broom against the house and said, "I've never been known for my housekeeping, as most Dutch people are, but one time, just before some people were coming to visit, I got busy and cleaned the whole place and even scrubbed the kitchen floor. It was just drying as our visitors came in, and they took one look and said, 'My, we heard you were not much of a housekeeper.' "

Before lunch, I was treated to a tour of the house. Scott told me later it took them three years to build it. They call it "the ninety–seventy house"—built in Scott and Helen's nineties and seventies.

When lunch was ready, Scott came in from cutting wood, and I met him at last. I had waved hello from the upstairs balcony; his sparkle and vigor had been visible even from there. At ninety-six, he still puts in his four hours of bread labor each day, often cutting and hauling wood, without benefit of chain saw or tractor.

After lunch, we went into the living room to talk. I wish I could reproduce for you here the whole conversation. It was delightful, it was interesting, and it was fragmented. When the Nearings talk, they bring in the history, the philosophy, the politics, the economics, the social changes that are directly or indirectly related to the primary topic. We touched on many things, but I had to select those parts of our conversation that fairly directly addressed their decision not to have children.

I had heard that Scott had at least one son. He had two children, it turned out—one born during his first marriage and one adopted during that same marriage. But he and Helen have had none. Scott's children were grown when they married.

Did they make a decision not to have children? Helen said, "Yes, because forty-five years ago, when we first met, it was bad enough to be living together, not to mention having children, without being married. My parents were horrified that we were living together, unmarried. At that time it was not done."

Were there other reasons they didn't have children? Helen again answered. "I think we were very enthralled with life together. We were having a very interesting life, traveling, studying; life was very full. It never entered my consciousness, really. There was no need to have children. Some people have children just to have something to look after or look after them, but I never needed either one. And since Scott had children, I felt he had no need to do so again. In a sense it was almost unspoken between us.

"As I said at lunch, and without fooling at all, I really believe in reincarnation, and I think I've had hundreds of lives and hundreds of children and will have many more lives and many more children. This is an interesting life without them. But I've enjoyed everybody else's children without . . . what's the word? Not envy, not regret. Without feeling badly that I didn't have them.

"I'm very glad, when I see some children, that I don't have *them*. As we have traveled through the United States, and we have done it plenty, I would say that there have been about a dozen children I would like to have had, out of the thousands I've seen. Most of them are badly brought up, they are spoiled, they are being brought up in a dreadful period in the history of the United States.

"I had a pleasant and very amicable family life. I had a wonderful life at home, got along very well with my parents, and fairly well with my siblings, and if children could have a life like that. . . . But I wouldn't want to be a youngster today. Our pleasures were simple, and what we asked for from our parents, what we asked for from life, was very little, and we had a fine time.

"I can enjoy a baby just as much as anybody. Children up to the age of six or seven are very sweet, but when they get to be older, unless they have been well-brought up, look out. We have found that if there are any well-brought-up children, in a pleasant, agreeable, amicable family, they generally have a European background.

"And then we have been in some dreadful American households where the children just monopolized the show. They break in on conversations, or have to have the TV on, or yell or scream. Dreadful."

We talked about how much it helps to have a model of good family life when you become a parent. Scott said, "Of my three sisters and two brothers, all but my brother Guy had children. He married, but he and his wife separated very soon, and he never married again. He lived a very self-sufficient, scholastic, experimental life. He was devoted to folk dancing. He was a scholar in Greek and Latin. He was a poet, and he was a botanist. He had plenty to fill up his time, and more." Helen commented, "He probably never felt the need for children."

Then she asked Scott, "Would you say that your brothers and sisters had satisfactory children?" He hesitated, then said, "So-so. It is a very unsatisfactory period of history. When a social system is disintegrating, coming apart at the seams, breaking down, it is not happy, you don't have a happy environment in which to grow up. And our social system has been going to pieces for about seventy-five years. It became an obviously outmoded social system about the end of the last century. I had seventeen years of the last century, and that was a century of normal growth and expansion. The rest of my life has been spent in a disintegrating, disorganized society."

I asked Scott if he could talk about being a parent and about not being a parent, since he has had both experiences in his marriages. "Yes," he said, "I have had lots of experiences." He seemed to be at the end of his answer.

Helen pressed him a bit. "Your parenthood was not particularly happy."

"Not particularly fortunate," he said.

Helen explained. "Scott's son did not go his father's way. Actually he went counter to him. At the end, there was a complete split. The son is dead now."

I asked Scott if he had held the same beliefs, been basically the same person he is now when he was bringing up his son, and he told me that he was. Helen commented that he had been gone from home a lot, with public work and lecturing, and that John, his son, had held that against him. But Scott said he thought John had a life "of his own making."

Helen and Scott spent the next few minutes talking about whether it is possible to influence children. Scott agreed that children can be influenced. He said that he devoted a great deal of time and thought to teaching the kids. One of them became a corporation executive, the other a successful banker. I asked Scott if he had taught them values that would run counter to that sort of material success.

"Well, I never taught them didactically. I taught them what was what, and left them to choose. You see, after a child gets to be about twelve or thirteen, gets to the point where he has a life of his own, a mind of his own, or her own, then all you can do is say, this is ABC and there is D, E, and F, and you can explain the situation. That's all you can do. You can't enforce. If you do, the kid will walk out. And then what do you have?"

I told him that some people say they should have children because they could produce a certain kind of human being, and the world needs that kind of person. Scott merely said, emphatically, "Un-uh!" I think he meant that people have chosen a very risky method if that is how they intend to change the world.

"I'm just writing a book now on the theme that life consists primarily of and is the result of social forces, and only incidentally of individual choices. We talk and act as if individual choices predominated, and social forces got in like mice through the wainscoting. Not on your life! Your life is pretty well set by society, and if you wriggle out between the fingers, you are doing very well."

I asked Scott if he felt as if he had wriggled out.

"Well, when I was living in the family, my own family, we ate on cut glass and silver; I went out and got a wooden bowl and wooden spoon." As he said this, he struck the table with his hand, so it went: "a wooden bowl," THUMP! "a wooden spoon," THUMP! "and chopsticks," THUMP! "and the silver and the cut glass were there side by side with my wooden utensils. And I lived that way. The kids and my wife made fun of me, and did all they could to bring me to my senses. But," he said with a twinkle, "it just didn't work. I did have something to say about my life. I did kick over the traces. But the lives of the youngsters . . ." He shrugged. "And if I had tried to control them (and it is a good thing I didn't try) it would have been no use. When a child gets to be an adolescent, he becomes, more or less, responsible for himself."

Scott told me that he is, first and foremost, a teacher. He likes children and gets along very well with them. "Whenever I get a chance, I teach. I set out very early as a teacher to have something to say about the society in which I lived."

"Until you got kicked out of school," added Helen. (Scott's formal career as a college teacher ended in 1917 when he was dismissed because of his political opinions and activities.)

"Since then, I've often been able to go into the schools, at the invitation of students, not at the invitation of the administration."

I asked both Helen and Scott to tell me a little about their childhoods and early experiences that might have had some bearing on their decision not to have children together.

Scott said, "I had a very useful childhood. There were six of us children, and my mother had enough money that she could have at least two servants in the house. She gave herself unremittingly to educating the kids. We were thoroughly educated at home, with tutors or governesses, and my mother read to us every day. Things were very stable, very dependable. My parents were not very dominant, but they were very exacting. The clothes we wore and the food we ate and the kind of company we kept: my parents were very arbitrary about that. We read the right books, met the right people, got up at the right time, went to bed at the right time.

"My mother was also a food reformer. She was born in 1864, when food was just being recognized as influencing health. We had lots of green stuff, fruit, plenty of vegetables, although she was not a vegetarian."

At this point, they gave me a copy of Scott's political autobiography, *The Making of a Radical*. Much of his early childhood is recorded in the first chapter. I read it immediately after returning from Maine. It gave me a much deeper understanding of how and why two such intelligent and thoughtful people would decide to spend the greater part of their lives homesteading.

The decision not to have children was a very small one for the Nearings, in that it did not involve much soul-searching. But Scott had already had children. It was Helen who would miss that experience if they did not have them. I asked her if she had expected, when she was growing up, to follow the traditional paths of marriage and children.

"When I was a child, I was pretty independent and off on my own, not like my brother and sister. For instance, when I went to camp (my first trip to New England) the other girls would get together and play or dance or sing or swim, and I'd go off in a canoe alone. Already at thirteen I was a loner. I've always been different from my brothers and sisters. They were not readers—we had a large library—but I had read all the books in the house by the time I was sixteen. I left home at seventeen to study the violin in Europe, and never really went home again." But she was in touch with her parents and they had a cordial relationship.

"Except when Scott and I went together. That was hard for them. Perhaps it was partly for them that I didn't push the issue of children."

Helen was twenty-six when she and Scott started living together. "I'd lived quite an unusual life in Europe studying the violin, and had traveled a great deal abroad. I had come back from Australia to see my parents, and I met Scott. He took the place of music, which had been my life up to then."

I asked her what that meant. "Well, I was a musician and that was my whole life, my major interest. I listened to and enjoyed good music; I played the violin and the organ a lot, and that has not been the case since we were together. What we were doing sort of precluded music. You can't mix concrete and dig ditches and play the violin. So it was a choice, not a hard choice at all, because I loved Scott and respected what he was trying to do and decided to team up with him." I said that she had certainly lived a different sort of life than she would have if she had stuck with music. "Unquestionably. But I have no regrets about that. Plus I still have the music, but not in a professional sense."

After living together for several years, and after Scott's first wife died, Helen and Scott married. Helen said, "I think I suggested it. By that time, I don't think it mattered much to either of us. But Scott was having a hard time, both politically and socially, and I admired him and wanted to share his name. Whether it was a good name or a bad name in society's eyes, I wanted to share it. That was the only sense in which it mattered to me."

I asked Helen if not having children was mostly a personal preference and mentioned what she had said earlier about her parents' feelings. "I think that consideration was mostly one of loving them and not wanting to hurt them, but if I had really wanted to have children, I would have had them. Like my liv-ing with Scott—I thought it was important, so I did it even though I knew it hurt them. If I had thought having children was important, I would have done that anyway, too. But I did consider the fact that it would be that much less worry for them if I didn't have children."

For Helen, the question of having children was "never para-mount. We were doing other things. We were freer to travel, to work. I was able to do much more with Scott."

Did she, at any time, think about wanting to have children? "No. Perhaps at the last, when I was about forty-three, when the period was really ending when I could, I looked at babies differently. I was quite human and thought it might be nice to have some little Scottinas running around, but I should say that was only at just the last possible moment, and was a very minor regret. But yes, there were moments when I would see babies and think, it's now or never. I wasn't stone cold to it."

Does she have any feelings about not continuing biologi-cally?

"No, because I think we are different souls. Are you familiar with Gibran's words? 'Your children are not your children. They come from life's longing for itself.' Take Scott's son, John: he couldn't have been farther from Scott in the end. In the beginning, he was of course a nice little boy, but later they were so far apart. He might just as well have been George Smith's son out in San Francisco, as far as Scott was connected with him.

"So, we might have had some very fine children or we might have had some more not so good. How can you tell? You don't perpetuate yourself. Scott was not perpetuated, in any sense."

I asked Scott what he thought about people choosing not to have children. "Well, there is an obvious relationship between now, when there are four billion people on the earth, and twenty-eight years ago, when there were two billion on the earth. In that quarter century, the population of the world has doubled. If the same thing continues, in twenty-eight more years, there will be eight billion people on the earth, so that in a period of about sixty years, there will be four times as many people. If that continues, we will very soon have standing room only. We are doubling the population every twenty-five years. That can go on for a certain length of time, but at some point it has to stop. Of course it will stop before that point, for various reasons—war, famine, pestilence, along with the voluntary decision against parenthood."

"What if every family had only one child?" Helen asked him.

"The population would diminish. In order to keep it stable, you have to have about two and three-quarters children per fertile marriage. You take the people who have had a high school education; their population is approximately static. They have about one and three-quarters children per fertile marriage. But the population is diminishing among those who have had a college education. They have about one child per fertile marriage." "Give everyone a college education!" Helen exclaimed. "That would certainly be a unique form of birth control."

What about the argument that people who are aware and educated should be perpetuating themselves in order to counterbalance all the people who are procreating mindlessly? Helen said, "Whenever I began to have thoughts like that, I remembered Scott's son, and that put it right out of my head. It is not really in your control what sort of children you will have."

Is it possible to bring up a child without the child becoming part of the society, adopting values that the parents disagree with? Scott's son sold war bonds, even though his father was a pacifist. Where did these influences come from? I asked. Scott said, "He got it everywhere. He got belief in the war (World War One) in school, from the other kids, from the news-

papers, from billboards. He got it from neighborhood gossip.
He was like the other boys. He didn't decide to be that way, he
was that way, and he didn't want to be any different. They sold
war bonds and he sold war bonds, which is the normal reaction
of a normal child."

Helen and I talked briefly about the unique experience of
carrying and giving birth to a child. "If I thought this was the
only life I was going to have, I might have acted differently,"
she said.

I asked Scott if he shares Helen's views on reincarnation. "If
you define reincarnation my way, yes. Life continues. All life.
Being continues. It changes form, every minute. The people
who try to make the world stand still," he laughs, "are doomed
in advance. They can't do it. The world moves. In the broad
sense of move. The universe in which I live is a very high-level
affair."

We talked about how little we know of the universe, how
inexact our knowledge is. Scott said, "We come from somewhere, we go somewhere. Whence and whither?" But he
thinks there is a consciousness that pervades existence. "People have for a long time said that there is a spirit of the mountain, a spirit of the river. Of course there is. There are spiritual
aspects of everything. The universe is a magnificent, worthy
enterprise, in which we participate. Part of it depends on us. If
we do our job well, it is worthy; if we do our job badly, we need
a kick in the pants for our failure."

I said that we don't have a very admirable track record at
this point, as a race. "No, the race is petering out, that is true.
Multiplying in number and diminishing in average quality.
And so much of the race at the present time is so indifferent."

At that point, Helen asked Scott to look at the fire, and he
said he would be delighted to. We discussed using that as a
break, but we all saw that the conversation was just about at an
end. While Scott was checking the fire Helen said that even if

they had had children, their own lives would have been much the same. "I think we could have lived the good life with a couple of children, but something else would have suffered— the building or the writing or the traveling. It might well have been worth it; but we considered it and decided not."

Later, two things about Helen and Scott Nearing occurred to me. First, Scott had talked about population considerations, but that wasn't the main reason either of them gave for deciding not to have children. Helen's statement seemed to sum up that decision: "We never felt the need; life was very full."

Second, they had said very little about the hundreds of young people who, through the years, have lived with them, worked with them, and been influenced by them. Helen and Scott Nearing provided those young people with a chance to try the good life firsthand. And countless other people have been moved to seek more healthful, harmonious lives because of reading the many books the Nearings have written. In these significant ways, Helen and Scott Nearing *have* had many children and contributed towards a saner, simpler world for us all.

8

Kathleen and Eric

Practicing Downward Mobility

KATHLEEN AND ERIC bought a huge old duplex with another couple, and now all four of them are living in
more space, more cheaply, than they had in rented apartments.
Each couple has total privacy, but the house is still a small
community.

The amount of living space allows two people to occupy it
without bumping into each other. That is important to both
Kathleen and Eric, who have rooms of their own as well as a
common room. All is neat, attractively put together.

Both Kathleen and Eric grew up in the western United
States; both finished college. They have been married for about
four years and are in their early thirties.

This conversation occurred in two parts. The first was alone
with Kathleen, the second with Eric for a while and then with
both people. There was no special reason for doing it that way.
We simply had some scheduling problems.

Kathleen began by saying, "I don't know the significance of
this, but I remember it vividly: My family and I were sitting at
the dinner table one night when I was fifteen or sixteen, and I
said that I was never going to have children. My father blew a
gasket. He got up from the table and stomped out of the room.

I guess he just could not understand how I could ever say that. And I don't know why I said that. I didn't know my head from a hole in the ground. I don't know if subconsciously I had been thinking about that and didn't want children or what."

Kathleen doesn't remember thinking any more about whether to have children until about five years later, when she was married to her first husband. "I was always of the point of view that I would not have children unless I was fairly well established, unless the marriage was good and the home was financially secure—all the arguments. I was never one to romanticize to the point of saying 'A child would be great and I'll figure out how to take of it later on.' But that marriage was very rocky; it was financially and emotionally insecure, so I had no thought of having a child at that time."

After several years, the marriage broke up; Kathleen went back to school and didn't think at all about having a child.

"And then I got involved with the population movement. That was about 1968 or '69 and that may have made me look at the question of childbearing. That and the women's movement, which came later. The population movement made me look at questions I had deep inside me. That comment I made at sixteen was obviously the result of something. I was also very involved in a lot of social movements at the time, and single again. I can't say that I made the decision never to have children then, but I was certainly looking at the possibility.

"The social implications of the population movement made me question why I wanted to have a child, when there are so many children in the world who don't have any parents. Am I really egotistical enough to want my own child, to have my own image created?"

I asked Kathleen if she had been assuming, up to then, that she would have children.

"Oh yes. Even then, though I was looking at the questions, I probably still thought that there was a good chance I would have a child. I don't think that was a major turning point."

It was during this time that Kathleen met Eric. They were both involved with Zero Population Growth, an organization which encourages people to have only two children, at the most, so that population will stabilize. They were friends for a long time before they became lovers and then eventually married.

"When we began living together, I didn't question it, but I had no inclination to have kids. I really liked kids, but I'm not sure whether I didn't feel any need for children or didn't feel it was right to have them. Those two things played together and I'm not sure which dominated. I think, though, that the decision started when we began living together.

"We talked about it. We talked about what we wanted to do in our lives and what children would mean. Eric made it clear that he had made a decision not to have children. That was pretty strong. But I still can maintain that it was my decision not to have them as well. If I had really wanted children, I'd have found someone else. I think there would have been other people I would have been compatible with who wanted children. I saw it as a separate decision, although it would have been difficult, because I loved him.

"The decision was consecrated a year ago, when Eric had a vasectomy. When he said, 'This is it. If you want a child, it can't be with me,' we knew that was our commitment not to have children.

"It was a long, long decision. And, before the vasectomy, I don't think it was ever so entrenched that we couldn't change our minds. It wavered from 90 percent sure one day to 50 percent the next."

Kathleen told me that she had been pregnant once, but at a time when she and Eric were still at a formative stage in their relationship. Because of that, and because she was in no position to provide for a child, the decision to have an abortion was a fairly easy one. She believes that the spirit of that child will continue, just as the spirits of all of us continue. "I believe in the lives of those who are living now and who should be taken care of now."

What if she had become pregnant after she and Eric married? "Maybe it would have been different. Maybe I would have had difficulty under those circumstances."

I asked Kathleen to tell me a little about her life and herself. Did she have a happy childhood?

"Absolutely. Mine was not an easy childhood—my father was somewhat of a maverick, in financial trouble at various periods of his life—but no matter how rough times were, there was always the sense, and there is even to this day, of my parents loving us and honestly wanting us to be there. There was never a moment when I doubted that. It may not have been calm, but I came away with a sense of security and love."

How have Kathleen's parents reacted to her decision?

"Well, they don't know it is a decision." She laughs. "If they read your book, they may. I mean, I don't care if you use my real name or not. We have never really discussed it, except my mother and I talked once. Her feeling is that if I don't want to be a mother, I shouldn't be. But I wonder how she feels about it emotionally. I am her only daughter and we are very close. But they don't know it is a decision. They don't know Eric has had a vasectomy. They probably figure I am not going to have children, because I am getting older and older and at some point it will simply be too late. I don't know how they feel, and Eric's parents don't know about our decision, either."

There has been no pressure from either set of parents.

"Maybe that is because we live two thousand miles away. That makes a big difference. If I were living in the same town, I might get a lot more of that. But we have severe problems just communicating with them. They are very angry, my father is, anyway, that we live so far away. That takes precedence over everything else. But they have never said anything, on either side. Eric's philosophy is so blatant that everyone knows. And everyone is going to chalk it up to population alone, which it is not necessarily.

"There are two elements in my philosophy. One is very personal: I want a certain kind of life. A life that allows me time to myself, what some people call a very selfish part of me. I want time to explore things, intellectually, emotionally, morally, socially, that I feel are important. And then there is the relationship with Eric. Both of us knew from the start that children were a heavy responsibility and did change people's lives together. We both like our relationship the way it is. I like my life the way it is. I have time for other children in my life, but they don't absorb my whole life. I feel I do better with the children I know because of that. And I feel no remorse about not having children of my own.

"The other side, and I have to give each side equal weight, is the social responsibility. I feel we need to have people in our society who are free of children, so that when a friend comes to me and says, 'please, take my child for a week, I need a rest,' I am a person who is free to do that because I don't have that heavy responsibility.

"But I also don't receive the love that the other person is getting. I have a different kind of love, but it is not the same as the love of a child for its mother and father."

She and I shared a vision of a society in which many kinds of lives are possible, accepted, and encouraged.

"Just as in the natural environment, life should have variety. I think there should be people who are living alone, who like it; people living in couples with no children, who like it; people with one child, with several children. I think if we had a society like that, which accepted all those possibilities, we could support each other much better than we do by assuming that everyone should have two children or any children.

"I think it would be a lie to say that I never feel a twinge of 'what would it be like to be pregnant?' That physiological experience. It is very difficult for Eric to understand that. My sister-in-law is pregnant now, and it is really exciting—I love to put my hand on her stomach and feel the baby kicking. But, as with any decision in life, you always give up something. Which is okay, too.

"When Eric and I were in the depths of our discussions about this, he would say, 'Well, there is a chance that when we are forty-five, we'll hit rock bottom.' I've talked to a lot of people who are going through the throes of the decision—they say that if they wait long enough, the decision will be made for them. But I couldn't live with that uncertainty. I have to make my own life and not leave those questions to chance. There are too many existential questions as it is, so make the decision and go ahead and live. Maybe when I am forty-five I *will* regret it."

I asked her if that would be a biological sort of regret, or regret over missing being a parent.

"Missing parenting, nurturing a child. You may throw out the whole interview with this remark, but I have not closed all the doors to taking care of a child. If someone close to me dies and there is a child, I would take responsibility for that child. Or I would adopt a child."

Kathleen and Eric go out of their way to have children in their lives. But they have had to overcome distrust from friends who say, 'Why would you want to have kids in your house since you have chosen not to have any? And why would anyone want to put up with kids if they don't have to?' Because they like to, on a limited basis. Close friends have come to believe that. But there have been a few upsetting scenes with people who are not good friends. One woman told Kathleen, "You are the most selfish person I have ever met," because she did not want children.

Unless Kathleen's brother's children need a home, full-time parenting is not something that they will choose in the near future, if ever. Their lives are full, and fairly happy, "except for those questions we all go through, like why am I here?"

"Maybe people like myself go through those questions and make it more difficult. If you believe that we are here to perpetuate the human race, then there is your ready-made answer. You can feel secure about that and go through life having had children without any questioning. But if you say, 'I'm not here to perpetuate the human race, there are plenty of people doing that,' then you ask, 'What the hell am I doing, what does it amount to?' When you have a kid, you know it amounts to that at least. For whatever it's worth, that person is probably going to be around when you are dead."

I asked Kathleen if she had any feelings of loss about her biological entity ceasing to exist. She said, "I think that is the worst idea human beings can have. We are so egotistical. Lower animals procreate because that is their instinct, but even nature reduces their numbers when it is obvious that they can't all survive. But we want *all* our images running around. No, I feel no regret, none at all."

Kathleen thinks she would be a good parent, possibly a difficult one, she laughs, because she is moody. "But I think I could nurture a child very easily.

"Kids are fun, and they are special. You learn about yourself and about life through them. It is a dimension in life that is marvelous. That is why not having them is a big trade-off. But I am trading one good thing for another. I can't quibble about that. But I do see the other side.

"It's funny to hold those two things in my mind: that children are a source of rich experience but also that you don't want them around all the time. I don't think it is a contradiction.

"I can't say that the decision itself was without its moments of pain, in terms of the idea of family. What is a family? Do two adults make a family? There are always children in a family, by the old definitions. And there are the trappings that go along with having a family. It certainly gives people something to talk about."

We went back, after talking some more about Kathleen's family, to the influence the women's movement had on her.

"I saw women blossoming. I saw myself as a woman blossoming, as someone with a broad horizon before her. Women can be lots of things, and it was really important for me to see that, and to grow intellectually as well as emotionally. To be really excited about ideas is not typically feminine in our society. And ideas excited me much more than childbearing.

"My sister-in-law argued with me that she didn't think it was right that people like Eric and me, who are healthy and intelligent and have good values, don't help perpetuate a healthy, intelligent race. She says it is the ignorant fools who should not have children. I said I thought that was very arrogant. That sort of attitude is too close to Hitler's idea of a super race for my tastes. And it is certainly not a good rationale for having a kid."

We talked a bit about men having vasectomies. I told her that I think something about a man having a vasectomy kind of evens things out. When a woman passes childbearing years, that's it for her. She can't change her mind. A man can father children most of his adult life. He can find a younger woman if he really wants to start a family. But if he has a vasectomy, they are on an even footing. Something in me likes that. She said, "I like the idea of men taking some of the responsibility. I'm pretty sick and tired of women taking the brunt of worrying about getting pregnant."

Another evening, I visited with Eric. He told me, "I first started thinking about not having kids as a result of getting interested in the population movement. But that is not to say that population was a major factor in my decision.

"I was not aware that people made choices about having children. I came from a middle class family and everybody had kids. My brother grew up and married and had kids. It was only when I got involved with the population movement that I saw it as an option.

"But I wasn't intimidated by other people in the movement, which I think happened to some people. Certainly there is a population component in my decision, but not because I think no one should have children. There are enough children around who need options open to them, as well as help. If I feel the need to help the next generation, there are plenty of them to assist.

"The decision didn't come at any one time. It came from thinking about population and about the needs of the next generation. What could most help them? Kids of my own would tend to divert my energies from assisting them as a generation to assisting two, or three, of their generation. I tend to think and work with society on a larger than individual level. Or did. Now (he laughs) the level is getting smaller and smaller. I don't think one is better than the other, but I work better on a larger scale.

"I didn't think I would be a terribly good parent. I mean, I think I would be fine—a normal, everyday parent. But parenting is becoming much more complicated than it used to be. Kids are exposed to a lot more. I think it is harder now. There used to be much more direction taken from society so that it was a little easier to stick your kids in school and do things. But people are trying to be more creative than that and, by necessity, have to be. It takes full-time or close to full-time energy to raise a child. It is a lot of responsibility to do that.

"I work well with children for two or three hours at a time. And I am not good with anybody who imposes on my time when I want my time. It is irrational to think that children will block their time out for adults, because they are children.

"I would probably be not only uncomfortable, but very difficult to live with, and unhappy, in that situation. I'm sure that when you have your own kid it changes. You become more accepting of all that, but you have to change a lot of things in your life. And the person who used to mean the most to you—your mate—now means maybe the most, but there is somebody else, and it is very easy for that new person to become the person who means the most. It changes the relationship with your spouse or your friend, whatever, and I was not prepared to deal with that, not know what the outcome would be until the kid was in the house.

"I have enough trouble giving Kathleen what she needs, just because I am the way I am. I'm fairly possessive of the time I want free. You are able to control your life a little more when a child is not needing you. There are plenty of people who are more talented at putting more energy into being parents than I am.

"I was pretty certain by the age of twenty-five that I wasn't about to have kids. But I decided that doing anything about it, like having a vasectomy, ought to wait. About the time I was thirty, we decided that I would have a vasectomy. We waited a year or two after that, and I had one last year. I have absolutely no regrets. I don't think you can ever be absolutely positive that you don't want to have kids and that you wouldn't have enjoyed them, though.

"Being a parent is an experience I will never know. On the other hand, I would have gone through twenty years of my life not experiencing what I will have by not having kids.

"From time to time, watching kids with their parents appears as romantic as all the picture books, and I realize it could be very nice. If you are a couple and you don't have a family and if you know a lot of people who do, then you are either out of step or something is missing. But those are flashes that last for twenty seconds.

"When I was growing up, everyone told me that I was intelligent enough and well-trained enough so that I could earn as much money as I wanted. But you may want to earn very little because that's all you can earn living where you want to live and doing what you want to do. That has been the case more and more with Kathleen and me. We have entered a trend of downward mobility. I would just not feel secure enough doing that with a child or two in the house. I'd have to find a job that could bring in some money so that I could save. I'd want to save for their education, for health, for a lot of things I now don't have to worry about. Our own old age is going to be hard enough financially. We have chosen to live the way we do. And it is not just a matter of absolute dollars. It is the worry, the making sure the money is there, making sure you are in a good community for schools and all that. We never did think we would earn millions, but now that we earn less and less, because that is what seems to make us the happiest, that has become pretty important."

I asked Eric to tell me a little about how he grew up, his family, his expectations. He said, "You know, one of the biggest subconscious influences on me was that my parents instilled in me a value system of doing things for other people, or at least being concerned about society. From the time I was in high school, I have been interested in environmental and social causes. That is how I first viewed population and whether or not to have kids.

"My home life was absolutely exemplary. I had the life that I thought everybody did, and I came to find out almost no one really did. I have two brothers, and none of us ever fought; we played together, did things together. My parents never yelled. You never heard anyone swear. We had council meetings whenever there was something to do with the family. Everybody got a vote and we did what the majority wanted to do, which usually tended to be a consensus.

"It was quite traditional; my father worked and my mother was at home. But since we were all boys, we did a lot of what has traditionally been called women's work. But there is nothing in my family life that would suggest it is not worthwhile having children. It has been that way for generations in my family. I had a great family life.

"My parents really set examples about what they considered right and wrong. But once they decided we were old enough to make certain decisions for ourselves, they would allow us to make the decisions and they would support us in them, whether they agreed or not. I think I appreciate this the most."

I asked Eric to describe his part in making the decision with Kathleen, or alone, not to have children. "I was definitely the first one. If she had decided to have kids, it would have been by someone else. I couldn't live with a woman who was into making babies, not because she wouldn't be nice, but because we wouldn't be together on it. Very early on I decided that if I made that decision, it would be based on things other than whether I could find a mate. If you go into a relationship, making that kind of a sacrifice of your own values, or of what you want to do with your life, you are starting on pretty weak footing.

"I've come across a lot of people who discovered they didn't want to have kids or thought they didn't but went ahead and had them and knew afterwards they didn't really want them. This was when I was working with population groups; there were a number of people around thirty-five who had already had their families. Then they discovered population groups and began to talk to other people about ways to bring up kids and whether or not to bring up kids at all. There were some people who did beautifully with their kids, but were very honest about saying they wished they had done something else. Which is pretty tough. But they were creative about being parents, so they probably had a maximum amount of time to themselves."

Eric described his own need for time. "I need to have it structured, by my structure, which is what makes having other people infringe on my structure a bit of a problem. It is not that I want a free-for-all time, like retirement, with no one bothering me. It is that I want to spend my time productively, for other people, and yet have some free time to myself so I don't go insane. Because I would like to do a number of things to benefit society as a whole, I have very little time for myself, really." Eric is currently working to demonstrate that there is a good, economical, nutritious alternative to most of what is available on supermarket shelves. He works for a food cooperative and is very involved in how food is grown and distributed and marketed in this country.

"In the long run, I would like to do more in the strictly environmental field. I want to be able always to have my hand in on a larger scale look at whatever is going wrong with the world, not because I think the larger scale is a better way to work on it, but because it is important to have a say in that larger picture from a local viewpoint.

"As long as there are human beings on earth, I would like to maximize the potential choices for future generations. We can't close their options by actions that we take. But more than that, and overriding that, I would like to maximize options for other life. Humans have already got more than most. I am not in the population movement because I think we are all going to hell in a handbasket. I'm in it because I think humans are far too dominant in the world. I have no particular love for the human race as a species. That doesn't mean I hate them. But it does not matter to me if the human species goes on *ad infinitum* or ends at some point. Maximizing the time that we are on the globe does not interest me.

"Biological continuation of myself is totally unimportant to me. I have never had any qualms about carrying on the line, or anything like that. Thinking about what a child of mine might look like is foreign to me. And I don't know why; it certainly is a logical emotional thing to wonder. But it is not so much that I don't wonder, as that the answer is impossible to know. Part of the reason I may not be very emotional about it is that most of my adult life this decision has been in the process of being made. So I have been thinking of it intellectually, as well as internalizing it, over a period of ten years. I may not be good at analyzing whether I am emotional about it or not.

"There are several ways of looking at the vasectomy. It does not negate the possibility of having kids. Only my own. If you are not hung up on that, then it is no big deal. But I would not like the vasectomy to be reversible. I mean, regardless of how emotional I get in my older middle years, I don't want to be able to make a decision to have a kid. Actually, I doubt very seriously that I would want to change my mind."

I said to Eric, "It sounds as if you rarely, if ever, seriously considered having children." He replied, "Once I realized it was an option, I rarely considered it." But I pressed him a bit, asking if there was ever a time when he really had thought about it. After a long pause, he said, "Yeah, I thought about it as I got closer to the vasectomy. I wondered if I wasn't just fooling myself, if I hadn't let all that population stuff go to my head. I think I satisfied myself that most of my reasons were not based on population problems. Some of the best reasons dealt with me personally, and with my relationship to society."

Eric has found other ways to satisfy much of what he sees as desirable about having children—things that are not good enough reasons to have children. He loves cuddling with children and likes to hold a child to feel its warmth and life. "One of the more interesting arguments for having children, which is (he laughs) not necessarily a good one, is to watch the development of another person. It is exciting because the whole process of life in any species is terribly exciting. Watching that develop is a great educational process. But it is also a very big responsibility. I think if you can do it all—taking care of what you need, your relationship with your mate, the necessity of making a living—and still raise kids in a creative way, which is pretty difficult, then that is an exciting thing. And I can see how exciting the kids who are close to me are, but I certainly can't see it as well as if they were my own kids, and I will miss that."

At this point, Kathleen joined us, and we talked a bit more. Eric asked her, "Do you have qualms about it now?" She was surprised that he would ask. He said that he didn't think she did, but wondered if there was just that little one percent of doubt. He said, "I'm not worried about it, but you can still do it, by someone else, if you change your mind."

I mentioned that for some couples, this is a real issue, especially if they are not monogamous. They may have to deal with a pregnancy by someone other than the husband. Some have solved this by having the woman sterilized as well. But Kathleen and Eric assured me that theirs is a monogamous relationship and will remain so for as long as they are together. Eric said, "I am not good at dealing with polygamy, except in theory. I can't give that kind of energy to two people. It is sort of the same as bringing up kids."

Kathleen agreed. "And you only have so much time during the day, and so much emotional energy."

Single
Nonparents

9

Closing Time Panic

The Thirties Crisis

TEMPUS FUGIT. It's very easy to arrive at your early thirties these days without having had children. The patterns which once led to early marriage and early childbearing are beginning to change. More women go to college, marry later in life, and establish themselves in the world of work. Or they stay single. Birth control information and contraceptives are widely available and acceptable.

It seems as if suddenly we find that our safe childbearing years are very limited. For possibly the first time in our lives, we seriously wonder, "Am I going to have children?" The timing of this question is pretty well set for women. It hits, if it hasn't before, in the early thirties, while there is still time to do something about it. The German word *Torschlusspanik,* "closing time panic," aptly describes what happens. It is now or never, and if never, will I regret it? Surely no one ever *really* regretted *having* a child.

What does the closing time panic mean? That differs, of course, for different people. You might see it as a last assessment of what having children might mean in your life. That it is truly the last chance to have children of your own is pretty overwhelming, when you think about it. Very few options are closed to us arbitrarily these days.

100

We can marry at almost any age, divorce, go back to school, learn a new job, write our first book, take up jogging, paint our first picture. But biology is arbitrary. It limits women to having their own children within the first forty-some years of their lives. Some people consider thirty-five to be the last safe year in which to have a child. Amniocentesis, which detects abnormalities of the embryo during the second trimester of pregnancy is extending those years somewhat, but the thirty-five to forty range is still just about it. Not only does fertility decline as we get older, it ceases completely at a certain point.

Finalities are always a little scary. Having children is also a finality. Once you have had children, you will never be able to live the life of a person who does not have children. Even if you are separated from them through divorce, you will still be thinking about your children, worrying about them, planning your free time so that you can visit them or they can visit you. It is never the same again.

Deviating from the usual and accepted way of life that most people live is a little scary, too. If you are married, you will be part of a very small minority if you don't have children. Almost everyone you know will have had children. The doubts, the feelings of loss, are inevitable. Let them come. "Why am I different? It must be pretty wonderful if everyone else is doing it. I don't want to be left out. Pretty soon it will be too late. There must be something wrong with me. My friends who have had children say they are glad they did."

Probably the feeling of being left out, of missing something important, is the most difficult to deal with. You will be standing on the shore, waving goodbye to all your friends who are headed somewhere else. You want to cry. "Wait! Take me with you. It's lonely back here."

Not only are you left on the shore, you are on alien territory. You will have to explore it yourself, with no maps. No one can help you, because so few people have lived the kind of life you are thinking of living. Married people have children. Women have children. We have received those messages in so many ways, on so many levels, it is difficult to go against them.

"Difficult, but not impossible," say the people in this book. If you are thirty and have not had children, remember that you have been doing fine without them so far, and you can continue to, if you want, in pretty much the same way for the rest of your life. In other words, find a better reason for having children than a temporary loss of nerve. They deserve better than being an antidote to fear.

This is not to say that you must decide, in this final reassessment, not to have children, just because that is a decision you made earlier in life. You may have changed. Your thinking may have changed. Your circumstances may have changed. You may have done the things you wanted to do and feel ready to go on to something else. You may have found the person you didn't think you ever would. Those *may* be good reasons for changing your mind.

But caution is needed. Look carefully at what has really changed besides your age. If nothing else has, you may be feeling twinges of closing time panic.

Men usually don't go through closing time panic, except for the last few days, or hours, before they have vasectomies. They often feel ambivalence about the finality of their decision. But there are two significant differences between a man's decision to end his fertility and a woman's biological cessation of ovulation. One, vasectomies can often be reversed. There's no guarantee, of course, but the possibility exists. Not so for a woman who has passed childbearing age. Two, having a vasectomy is a voluntary action. Women can do nothing to stop the end of their fertile years.

Many of my friends and acquaintances who are in their early thirties are having their first babies. Some of them had said earlier that they were not going to have children. What happened?

Some, I'm sure, simply felt ready to have children for the

first times in their lives. Some had gone from bad marriages to ones in which they felt good about having children. For a few, who married late, it was the first time they had looked at the question of children in the context of a relationship with a beloved mate. Perhaps some succumbed to the "closing time panic."

Maybe it was the first time they had ever felt any deep urges to have a child. One night at a gathering of friends I spoke with one of the men about the "to have or not to have children" question. He told me this story: For most of his adult life, he had been responding with indifference, frustration, and even contempt to the question, "I wonder what my child would look like, be like?", which seemed to entrance other people. "What was the big deal? It didn't interest me at all," he said.

Then, one day about a year ago, the woman he was with at the time said, "I wonder what our child would look like." She then began describing their child. He said, "I totally freaked out. I mean, it suddenly dawned on me how much I had been repressing, and that is the word for it, repressing those feelings about *my child*. Suddenly, for the first time in my life, I understood what other people had been talking about. I was completely taken by surprise by the strength and depth of my feelings towards this dream-child. What *would* he or she look like?"

Another story: One of the women I interviewed for this book, who had trouble understanding what all the fuss was about at the office when someone had a baby, told me recently that she, too, finally understood how it feels to wonder about your child. She recently separated from her husband and is seeing another man for the first time in years. "I looked over at him and suddenly I had the thought, what would it be like to have a child with this man?" At last she had understood; she felt the intense curiosity which had been alien to her before.

This raises again the question of where those feelings come from. The two people who described these experiences both said that the feeling was spontaneous and almost overwhelming in intensity. Neither had ever before felt it. Both had even been contemptuous of other people who described such feelings. The woman said, "I was sure they had just been conditioned to feel that way. Now I'm not so sure." In her case, though, this wellspring of feeling won't result in parenthood. She was sterilized several years ago.

Such feelings obviously are not good enough reasons to decide to have children, but I begin to see how people make decisions in the midst of them. It is a kind of emotional strike-while-the-iron-is-hot decision. I've read articles that say deciding to have a child requires discontinuing birth control measures, because the practice of birth control is so prevalent. Those articles also report that many people have difficulty taking active steps to become parents. But, given an easy way to have a slip-up, they will do so.

In the midst of a bout of intense curiosity about "our children" or good feeling about our partner, many of us have strong pulls towards deciding to have children, even if at other times our reason tells us we don't really want to. It may be that during those times we are most likely to forget to take a pill, put in a diaphragm, use a condom. And so we let ourselves have that accidental pregnancy, because a strongly ingrained part of us says that it is the natural and instinctive thing to do, in spite of our intellectual protests to the contrary.

Whatever that feeling is, it's powerful, and we don't know much about it. It may be instinct. It may be that certain circumstances or combinations of things bring it out. Both people I cited were in the midst of good love affairs, possibly of a kind they had never before experienced. This is not to say that only certain love relationships cause us to feel curious about or interested in our unborn children; but maybe that happens for people who have buried those feelings for years.

That feeling may be built in by nature so that the human race continues. I doubt, however, that any cavewoman turned to her mate and said, "I wonder what our baby will look like." Probably the awareness of that feeling is taught through our nurturance in families. Does any new baby escape being compared to Mommy or Daddy or Uncle Jeff or Aunt Sally? I wonder if ancient people also said, "He has your eyes," or "She has your nose." I think they did.

To see physical characteristics passed from generation to generation is a beautiful part of life—beautiful and compelling in ways we only vaguely understand. Even more compelling is seeing the child so accurately mirroring the gestures, inflections, phrasings of the parent. Narcissistic? Yes! Powerful? Absolutely.

No wonder then, that even the most dedicated nonparents have their moments of doubt, their feelings of loss. At times, to be childless is to look into the mirror and see nothing. This is not the same as feeling that you are nothing. It is to be alone in time, without even your own image for company. You face the void. Sometimes we find it hard to trust our ideas that continuance of life, of humanity, is what counts. Something in us longs to continue as us. We want our very selves to go on in some form, in ways that we suspect might be important.

Whence springs this fear of ending, this impulse to continue? Is it a mere survival mechanism, suddenly obsolete, left over from when our small numbers put survival in question? Is it "life's longing for itself" or the something in us that does not love the waste of any potential? We don't know.

The message that we should want to have children and "really ought to" is deeply ingrained in human society. If there is a biological counterpart, to go against all that is more than most of us have been willing to do. Easier to let nature take its course, to have that experience, to share in the destiny of our mothers and our sisters from time immemorial. Who are we, after all, to question so powerful an urge?

I don't intend to speak badly of those who respond to that urge by having a child. I am acknowledging that once you feel it resisting is very difficult if you are at all able to have a child. None of us are totally without ambivalence, but surely we can find better answers to the question, "Why have a child?" than "Why not?"

In her book, *Silences*, Tillie Olson speaks about the conflict between having children—being a mother—and any kind of creative work which requires concentration and full focus. I recommend it to anyone who is considering an art form as a life work. What I do requires absolute concentration and hours without interruption. Tillie Olson is a mother and an artist. She has done a masterful job of describing both.

We have all heard all the arguments. You can put your children in day care while you write or paint at home. You can rent a studio or an office and go to work away from home. You can hire household help. You can share all the housework and child care with your mate. If you can afford the rent, the help, the loss of other income, that is. If your mate is willing, that is.

Many women work, have children, keep their households running and somehow still manage to enjoy life. I don't know how they do it; I have a lot of respect for them. I still think that something has to give.

The question so often comes back to one of self-knowledge. If you want to do something, you probably will find a way to do it. Just remember that everything you do costs you something in time and energy. If you choose well what you do, based on what you know about yourself, the returns will probably prove to be worth it.

I have no way of knowing if having children might become more important to me during the next couple of years. But that does not matter right now. What matters is that I have decided to live my life in the present moment, doing things for the future only if they are also good for today. And planning to someday have kids is not good for my today.

One woman I interviewed raised an issue related to the thirties crisis that I hadn't even thought of. She said, "I know so many women who, when they got to be around thirty, even if they had decided not to have a kid, suddenly decided they were going to have a child. There often was no man really involved: they were just going to get pregnant by some poor schlep who didn't know what was going on. Talking to them, what I think I hit on was the 'beat the clock' thing. In all of our cultural anxiety of aging and losing one's youth and one's sexuality there is that question, if you aren't beautiful and sexy, what are you? It's easy to answer if you can say you are a mother. I saw these women deciding to take themselves out of the race before time and the effects of aging took them out of the race. They were getting away from the sexual role, into the motherhood role.

"And these were no ignorant women. These were women who had good educations and were articulate and yet I saw them responding to all this conditioning. I don't have kids, and sometimes I see men wondering how to respond to me. It's as if there is this question in the air, 'What kind of a woman denies her motherhood?' "

A better way to put the question might be, "What sort of woman makes conscious choices about her life?" The next five chapters are five unique answers to that question.

10

Deborah

On Not Liking Children

FROM THE TIME I was twelve or thirteen and started thinking about having children, I thought it might be kind of
nice, but I knew I wouldn't want to do it for a long time!"

Deborah says she leads a double life. In town, she is an attor-
ney. At home in the country, she is a keeper of animals, a gar-
dener, a jeans-and-boots lady who likes to muck around in the
dirt. You might call her a gentlewoman farmer.

I visited her one day after a night of pouring spring rain. The
sun was beginning to come out and all the greens were brilliant
and sparkling. Deborah's house is enviably situated in a valley
surrounded by mountains, mountains far enough away to let
in lots of sun. The house is large for one person, but until recently Deborah shared it with a partner. She owns the house.
Down the hill is a small barn where Deborah keeps her horses.
Across the way is a garden plot, partially planted.

Deborah is thirty-three and has never been married. She is
not sure she will ever marry. She likes renewing the commitment to her partner each day. She sees no reason for marriage
unless she wants to have kids.

Although Deborah was born in a city, her family moved to
the country when she was quite young. Hers was a happy child-

108

hood. Her parents, who still have a loving relationship, had a traditional marriage—he made the living and she raised the kids. Deborah thinks her mother's not working was a matter of the times and the family's financial circumstances. She describes her mother as "very independent."

When Deborah began dating, she assumed that she would marry some day and have children. But then she "was not thinking about the reality of it." She vividly remembers her father commenting that he would not go out with someone he wouldn't marry. For Deborah, that was the point at which she began to realize that it was possible to enjoy lots of different people without being together forever. She also began to consider that perhaps life was possible without marriage. Both her parents were from the South; they were much more formal and traditional than she is now.

At college, there were lots of group discussions about the tension between wanting a family and wanting a career. But Deborah rarely, if ever, attended these seminars. She said, amazed at the memory, that she "couldn't see any conflict then." By the time she was a senior, though, she was beginning to realize that she possibly didn't want "a standard family and children." But she had not made up her mind.

She laughingly told about her few baby-sitting experiences, saying that she hated it. And when people would ask her when she was going to get married, she would tell them, "Not for a long time."

Then, a few years ago, she found out that she had an ovarian cyst that would require surgery. Her doctor assured her she would still have at least one functioning ovary, so she would still be able to have children. She told him, "But I don't want to have children." It was the first time she articulated her decision. The doctor said that of course they were not going to foreclose that opportunity, because chances were she would change her mind. Deborah was angry. "It seemed to me I could make up my own mind."

She has not yet had the surgery, but eventually it will have to be done. Even if it doesn't involve both ovaries, Deborah will probably take that opportunity to be sterilized, mostly to simplify birth control. During the past few years, she had been living with a man who had had a vasectomy, so selecting a method of birth control was not a worry for her.

I asked Deborah if she could trace how she came to the decision not to have children.

"There are a lot of different threads. One is that I don't like children, and I'm lucky that I grew up in, developed in, a milieu in which it was all right not to like children. It's not that I hate them—I just don't feel like cooing over them. I discovered that I wasn't a social outcast when I said I didn't want to be around children.

"I find children in general to be extremely demanding. Part of that is that they have not been socialized. It's demand, demand, all the time. Me, me, me. I find that very irritating.

"My mother, who wants grandchildren, says that my animals are a child substitute, and maybe they are; sure, they are dependent, but if I don't want to deal with them, I just put them outside.

"I don't find children to be charming and appealing. But I think the experience of actually giving birth, especially consciously, being involved, would be a fascinating and wonderful experience. That's really the only part of having children that appeals to me."

I asked Deborah how she feels about children once they have become people who can respect other people's needs, saying, "They do reach that point eventually."

"I guess they do, but I'm not positive they reach that point with their parents. I know they do with other people.

"It's really hard for me to understand why people have children. I guess I'm that far on my side of the issue. Of course there are a lot of clichés about why people have children—they want to reproduce themselves, they don't know what else to do with themselves—I have no particular desire to reproduce myself. I like myself, but I don't need another me around.

"I have a lot of things I do with my life—my life is very full. I don't have an empty spot that needs to be filled. I presume that's one of the reasons people have kids, but I think it's very hard to get an honest answer if you talk to people who have kids about why they did it. They have already committed themselves. Everyone wants to be a perfect parent and no one wants to admit they resent it. But I'm not sure what the reasons are for having children."

I said that it sounded like there may not *be* any good reasons for her to have children. She agreed. I asked her to describe herself.

"I am, among other things, a compulsive worker," she laughed. "And I have close friendships. I love animals. In general, I'm quite happy with myself. The man I was living with for five years left a few months ago, so I've been making a lot of adjustments. Obviously, my life is not as full as it was, but I'm sure it will be again.

"I like a fair amount of time alone. I suppose I take an almost neurotic pleasure from my self-sufficiency." It isn't that she does not take a lot of pleasure from her relationships with people. She does. But she also loves knowing that she can take care of herself, even under very difficult circumstances.

"And it is not just physical, logistical kinds of things. It's also learning to rely on my own emotional resources and not to have to have, though it is much nicer to have, that kind of leitmotif of support you have when you are living with someone. That's really important. A friend of mine, years ago, said that it is terribly important to learn to live alone—not that you have to do it, but so you know you can."

What other things influenced her decision not to have children?

"This decision has been evolving for a long time. That conversation with the doctor was just the light bulb over the head,

the epiphany. The man I had been living with had four kids
and frankly he didn't want kids either. He couldn't say that
about his own kids, of course. But that was an influence, of
sorts. I think the demandingness of those kids was part of what
made his marriage fall apart, although there were lots of other
factors.

"There's a lot of stress, financial as well as emotional, for a
man in a traditional family. But the financial aspect of having
kids is not one that I've really thought about. I've never been
that close to deciding to have kids. My thinking has been more
personal and emotional."

I asked if the women's movement had any effect on her decision.

"Definitely. Part of it is that the women's movement created the culture that makes it okay to decide not to have kids.
You don't have to go around pretending you are sterile.
Part of what was going on when I was in college, which was
before the women's movement, was that there were just so
many capable, energetic women around and it was so obvious,
you didn't have to talk about it, that there were lots of things
you could do in this life besides have children. I'm sure that
shaped my decision a lot. If I had gone to a different school, or
if it had been a different time, when it was just assumed you
would be a wife and mother, I don't know—I don't think I'm
such a strong independent thinker that it would have had no
effect on me.

"I didn't get involved in a lot of discussions about it because
it just didn't seem to be a concern. It just didn't occur to me
that I had to think about those things at that time. I was learning things and having a good time, and I wasn't starting to live
my real life—I was getting ready for it!

"I was involved a lot with the civil rights movement, and so
I did have some contact with kids. I did some tutoring and
those kids were okay, but I have just never had a feeling that I

wanted to have kids. It is a whole lot more than just giving birth, and I'm not willing to put up with what comes later."

I asked Deborah if her family knows about her decision.

"I guess they know. I think they know that my sister, who is older than I am, she's thirty-six, wants to have children, but she just hasn't set up her life so that she has any. I could analyze her situation and say that she doesn't really want to have children, but she is much more ambivalent than I am. If she had had a real desire to have kids, she would have done so by now. My mother does want to have grandchildren, and she does give a hint now and then. She can't imagine that I don't want to have children. We discuss it from time to time. How does she put it? You can't be a full human being unless you have children. I think you can. I don't feel it as pressure, though, because that kind of decision is mine, and she knows that. She is just kind of trying.

"My sister says that she is really sorry I don't have kids, because she would much rather have nieces and nephews than kids.

"Another thing that may have solidified my decision is that I have friends who have perfectly horrible children. The kind of kids, who when their parents have come over to your house, try to get everyone's attention, all the time, in the most obnoxious ways—I don't think there is any way to do that charmingly. I finally told them they should get a grant from Planned Parenthood, just to go and visit people with their kids.

"There really aren't any kids in my life. Although in all the houses you see along this road, all the women are pregnant, except for a woman who's about seventy and me. (she laughs) So I guess there are going to be a lot of little kids around here. There are a couple of kids up the road, and I find them, frankly, to be a royal pain. Actually, they aren't too demanding, but when I'm out fixing the fence, they come and ask questions. That's okay for about five minutes, but then I've had enough.

"I think there was a time when I had difficulty putting up with any other person's needs. And I've gotten beyond that. When you live with someone, obviously their needs have to be very important to you. Or it doesn't work. At least the man I was recently involved with was a source of satisfaction for me. I enjoyed doing things for him, just as he enjoyed doing things for me. Obviously there were times when we said, 'Go to hell,' but I think an adult's needs are much different than a child's. It's much more a matter of choice, a day to day choice. If it becomes too much for you, even for reasons that you aren't proud of, you can abandon an adult relationship. I think that having children is the only commitment you can make that is irrevocable.

"Even if there is a divorce, if you are a woman you can't count on not getting the kids, even if you don't especially want them. I have some friends who got married only on the condition that if they got a divorce, the kids would go to him."

Any other influences?

"One that is quite recent, in terms of making me feel more confident that I have made the right decision, is reading *The Women's Room*. The first two hundred pages of it are what the author self-consciously refers to as soap opera, the day-to-day lives of women whose husbands go off to work while they stay home and clean up the house and take care of the kids. Some people I know were just unable to read those first two hundred pages, it was just too boring, they couldn't handle it. But most of the people who couldn't read it were people who stay home and have kids and take care of them. It really points out the baby trap.

"Here are women who were madly in love with some guy when they were eighteen or nineteen. They get married, have kids, and lose their relationships with their husbands. Their life is focused on the kids. They feel that they are attached to what is real in this world, bringing up kids, and their husbands are just support characters."

"It doesn't have to be that way," I said.

"No, of course it doesn't. In fact, none of my friends have lived that way. But it was in the course of reading that book that I have ever had any sympathy for women in that situation. I thought they had made that choice, but they didn't know what they were getting into.

"I know some of my friends have kids and jobs and all, and they seem to manage it, but I think you have to really want it. I think a lot of it is energy level, and energy levels are exercisable. They are like muscles; you can develop them. I don't ever want to say that there is anything I can't do just because I've chosen to do other things. You can develop your energy level, you can learn to get some space, even in bits and pieces. But you have to want something a lot."

Deborah mentioned that she is now considering the question of having or not having animals. They take relatively little time and energy, but even that is too much if she is not really getting much enjoyment from them. For her, that question centers on energy level. Does she want to work at increasing her energy or not? She knows that she now likes to get home from work and do something relaxing instead of something that takes intense effort. "It's not just a matter of patience, either. It's the difference between having something that must be done, whether you feel like it or not, or doing something only when you want to.

"I really don't have any regrets. I've been searching inside myself and I really can't find any. Part of it is that, at bottom, I'm really too self-centered to have kids. I like the way my life is now, and I really don't want anyone intruding on that. But sometimes I wonder if I am kidding myself. The mainstream still says that you are supposed to have a child and I'm a product of that culture. You are looked at oddly if you don't have them. But right now I can't find any regrets. I can't magnify the fact of having to pay school taxes to the level of a regret."

Deborah went through a period when her reasons were political as well as personal. "I was deeply involved in the civil rights movement and the anti-war movement, and I really believed at the time that the world was a disaster and that it would be immoral to subject anyone to it." But now personal preference is the main reason Deborah is not having children.

"You have problems with some people not understanding your decision, because the mainstream grows up, marries, and has kids, even if it doesn't work out, that is what they are doing. One thing I also feel from some of my neighbors, especially, is that they feel sorry for me. 'Poor lady, there must be something the matter with her.' "

On marriage: "I've seen a lot of people who seemed to feel trapped because they were married. And I've seen a lot of commitments not really be commitments. I don't think my personal relationships are anyone else's business. It's kind of an apolitical objection to marriage."

I said, "Not to commitments?"

"I think I do have difficulties with commitments. I've often said that when I planted asparagus here, that was one of the biggest commitments I ever made! But, probably my feeling about commitments has a lot of bearing on my decision about not having children. Obviously, people change, and grow a lot, all the time, and if I liked children, it would create real problems for me. I know that I have gone through a lot of change in my life. I certainly wouldn't want to be stuck with a decision I made the way I was ten years ago. Therefore it's probably a good thing I never had kids. Even if I really liked kids, I would still be afraid that the detractions would be more than the attractions, because I really love my work and where I live.

"I think if I had not had animals, I might have had kids! On two levels: It helped me to understand my limitations in responding to unarticulated needs; and watching them change and grow, seeing positive results, made me feel good without having excessive demands made on me."

I asked Deborah if she thought that being a parent changed people in any way.

"It brings out qualities in them that are nice, but changes their focus very much. For some of my friends, having kids has interfered in some ways with their relationships with other people. There is family-life growth rather than other kinds of growth. I feel very angry when I hear people express the position that having children is morally superior to anything else there is to do."

After Deborah and I ended our conversation, we took a walk together, up the hill behind her house. We looked for wildflowers, and found a few. The blueberry bushes were profuse. After our walk, we sat talking in the sunshine. I stayed until the shadow of the mountains reached the house and as I drove home, I wished a little that the issue were as clear for me.

11

Naomi

Protecting Her Children by Not Having Them

"I FEEL LIKE it was only when I was thirty-seven years old that I stopped struggling just to survive."

Naomi. Her house is full of lived-in furniture, books, hand-made things lovingly chosen, lovingly used. The best room in the house is one she made out of a sun porch. Behind the house, the hill drops steeply and a little brook gurgles below. The wood stove was cheerful on the rainy night I visited.

Naomi put candles on the table for the good, impromptu dinner she prepared. "There was a time," she said, "when I wouldn't have dreamed of fixing a meal for someone without a big meat dish and without a lot of planning. But now it feels all right just to share whatever I have." It felt fine to me.

Naomi is a large, strong-looking woman of forty-four. She is wonderfully warm, responsive, and articulate. She comes from a poor, non-nurturing family, and has spent many years working hard at overcoming the effects of that background. She is single, has never been married, and teaches psychology at a nearby college. We spent a long evening talking about how it happened that she had no children and how she feels about her life.

"Well, I don't really remember when I became conscious

118

that I wasn't going to have any children. There was not one specific time when I said to myself, 'Okay, now that's true.' "

Naomi laughingly says she did a lot of thinking about having or not having children during the fourteen years in which she was in and out of analysis with three therapists. The first was a man she saw for two years; the second was a woman she saw for over five years; the third was a man she saw for about a year and a half.

The discussion with her woman therapist, whom she began seeing right after she turned thirty, quickly came to the time-loaded question of children. "If I had wanted to get married and have children, I'd better have been at it, because my time was running out." The closing time panic was not yet a factor for Naomi, but her therapist was feeling it for her.

"I remember talking with her about my difficulty in getting along with men and having relationships with men. It was sometime during that five years with her that it began to become clear that I was not going to have children. That was a major issue for her. She was married and she was pregnant with her third child while I was seeing her, and she very clearly considered being married and having children a part of being mature. I always wonder if I am remembering this correctly, but my recollection was that she viewed it as a sign of growth if I would be able to do that."

Eventually, this attitude caused problems in their relationship, and Naomi saw that she was becoming a different sort of woman from what her therapist was. "That was a problem and a very painful one for me, because she was like a good mother for me. It was really she who enabled me to become a woman. But then I turned out to be a woman very unlike her and that was very hard."

Naomi and her therapist spent a year and a half painfully disagreeing, parting, and not knowing they were parting. After ending her sessions with that therapist, Naomi began seeing her third therapist, a "very warm, wonderful, loving man. I wouldn't have used the word at the time, but he was genuinely a feminist. He was the first person in my entire experience, and I was then thirty-five, who was totally, genuinely, and positively accepting of me as I was."

Her psychiatrist had worked at an institution for deserted, neglected, rejected kids who had no place else to go. "He spent his whole life working with kids who essentially were not wanted. I remember saying to him one day, with great feeling, I remember this very vividly, 'I really want to have a baby, but I don't want to raise a child.' And he said, with a great sigh, from the very bottom of his being, 'If you only knew how many people feel that way and don't have the wisdom not to do it.'

"He was the person who gave me the most affirmation and the most reassurance; he was also the person who was able to say to me, at another time, 'When are you going to come to the point when you recognize that you are a strong, capable woman, see that as an asset, stop being afraid of that, and start using it in all the positive ways it can be used?' "

Naomi doesn't even like to think about what her life might have been like without this affirmation. "He also said to me one time, when we were talking about my being single, 'Has it ever occurred to you how much integrity has been involved in your decision?' Those were two words I'd never looked at. I had not seen it as a decision, and it didn't look like integrity to me.

"He said my independence was very important to me. I don't know how he said it, but the essence of it was: 'Your integrity, your self, is important to you, and you've not been willing to compromise that. And in your life situation, marriage would have been a compromise, for reasons which for you are sound and valid.' That was a whole new perspective on my singleness. And my childlessness."

Naomi's therapist died in 1971, at a time when support for being single and for being childless was still very hard to find. But she did have other sources of support in a "strong network of people, most of whom were single women, either divorced or never married. That network was a long time in building, and it was very strong. Some of us had never married and we felt differently about it from person to person and from time to time.

"I talked to a friend of mine last night who is exactly my age who told me the thing she is working on most at this point is finding a close and intimate relationship with a man because she is certain at forty-four that that is what she wants more than anything else. I hope she finds it, but she won't have children either at this point in the game.

"Other people, like my sister and friends of mine who did have children, who were left to raise them by themselves because their men left them, for whatever reason, have been very reaffirming about my decision not to have a child. They were very clear about how painful it is to have a child and be unsupported in having one.

"One of the reasons why I feel very good about not having children is because my sister did, and because I've had a niece who is now close to twenty with whom I've had a very close relationship all her life."

There was a time when that relationship was cut off—"an adolescent period when she wanted nothing whatsoever to do with me"—but that ended as Naomi's niece matured and they again became close friends. They spent last summer together, an important time for both of them.

"I know that I feel very strongly about what it has meant to me to have a child in my life. I think not having had children would have been a very different experience if there hadn't been an important child in my life. That would have been a terrible loss. I really had the best of both worlds. I had a child whom I could have when I wanted and then I could take her back home when I didn't want to be around her any more. I was also very fortunate in that my sister, who, as I said, was left alone with her child, deeply and genuinely appreciated sharing her child. So there was no jealousy or resentment when I would take Kimberly off her hands for a while. And though she is my sister's child I do feel that I've played a fairly major role in her development."

During most of those years, Naomi and her sister lived close enough so that frequent visits were fairly easy. In fact, Naomi was in the delivery room when her niece was born and helped take care of her for the first month she was home from the hospital.

"It was very hard at the time," she says, "because I was twenty-six, and I certainly had not resolved whether I was going to have children of my own, and here was my 'little' sister, (and she is considerably younger than I am) having the baby and I was washing the diapers and making the soup instead of having my own baby so that she could breast feed her baby every two hours."

From the time Kimberly was about two, visits have been frequent and friendly. "That was very special and still is." Kimberly's childhood has not been an easy one. There have been problems with her father and between her parents. During some of those difficult times, Naomi and Kimberly spent weekends together, went camping, had large chunks of time together. I told Naomi how lucky her niece has been to have another important, caring adult in her life, and Naomi told me that Kimberly has expressed that. "When she was a little kid, she would say, 'Boy, I'm lucky to have an aunt like you.'

"My woman psychiatrist said once, and I have never forgotten it because I think she was absolutely, unerringly right, 'You're protecting your children by not having them.' There is a lot of truth in that; I feel strongly that if I had had a child any time in my twenties or early thirties, I probably would have been a child abuser. Certainly I would have resented that child a lot of the time. And all of that is based on the assumption that I would have had that child essentially by myself. It's very important to understand that, because it's very hard for me to even imagine having a relationship with a man whom I trusted enough, felt was stable enough, supportive enough, to stay with me through the responsibility for that child. That is not part of my experience.

"I make the assumption that women essentially raise children by themselves. And that's irrational, it's not even factually based, because I know lots of people for whom that is not true. Like my friends who were just here for two days. They weather all kinds of trauma, and they are really, clearly in this together. But somehow, in my own perception I was never able to visualize that."

Naomi's father left his family when Naomi was fourteen and stayed away for three years, returning when she left for college. He is still there. But the lack of his physical presence was not what Naomi felt most painfully.

"I was never able to feel him there emotionally. It's ironic and I don't understand it at all, because of my two parents, my father's affection was much more clearly expressed. When I talk about whether or not my parents loved me, it's always reasonably clear to me that my father did. It's never clear to me that my mother did. It's not that she didn't love me, but that she wasn't capable of loving, which is different.

"But my father loving me is different from his having been there for me, because he never was there for me. In my mother's many and varied attacks on me, he didn't defend me. He somehow was never able to counteract the destructiveness of her attacks on me. And I couldn't go to him, couldn't talk with him, so he was not an emotional support, even though he cared for me. That's a distinction which is very important, because I learned from him that you can't count on men on an emotional level—I feel that. It is only now, at forty plus, that I'm beginning to learn that indeed there are some men you can count on at an emotional level. I'm sure that's been an important factor in my never having children."

I said, "You feared that you would have to do the emotional

nurturing of a child by yourself? That no man would do any of it?"

"Or of me. *Me*. I don't think I was even looking far enough ahead to think about whether he would nurture a child. I was thinking about whether he would nurture me. And unfortunately, that's been my experience with men. That's partly because I haven't had the capacity to choose very good men. But I think it's also because it is hard to find men who can be emotionally supportive and nurturing. I think given what I had to choose from in my generation . . ."

In the fifties, the roles were pretty clearly defined. The important responsibilities of the world were given to men.

Naomi said, "I came out of a generation of chauvinists. You were the little woman and he was the big man. My last therapist once said to me, 'You're just not going to be anybody's little woman.' "

Her decision, made early and unconsciously, slowly became apparent to Naomi. "I punished myself for years over my failure to marry, to have a man. But even when I was punishing myself brutally and horribly and awfully, there was some part of me that knew there was no way I was going to compromise that self, however high a price I paid. For a long time, I have paid a very high price, but ultimately, I think I have paid a far lesser price than many of the women who did marry and have children. I know, because as I get older I realize that the choices I have made have been good choices for me. While those choices did involve certain losses, nevertheless they have not involved a lot of compromise. They are choices I can live with very comfortably at this point."

I wondered, aloud, where in the world that absolute unwillingness to compromise, to marry, to follow the expected path, had come from. Naomi didn't know. None of her therapists knew. She says, "When I look at where I've come from, I'm a pretty miraculous case."

Where did she come from? What kind of home?

"I never think of my parents as being in a traditional kind of marriage, because I never think of my parents as being traditional people, although they certainly fit the pattern where the father earned the money and the mother stayed home with the children. But my parents were not educated people. Neither of them went beyond eighth grade. They were poor people, very poor, very hardworking. My father was a hard and steady worker. My mother had been very deprived as a child. She came from a huge farming family with a dozen kids and no money and she obviously never got any real attention or affection. I don't think it was that nobody cared about her; I just think my grandmother didn't have any time for her. She was far too busy to give much real caring to anybody. My sister and I have debated a lot about my mother, about whether she is retarded, whether she is socially deprived."

One therapist told Naomi that her mother's emotional adjustment sounded as if it was at about the level of a three year old. Naomi agreed.

"She is totally self-centered. She has no ability to differentiate anyone from herself. No one in her life has any existence, in her conception, apart from her. You exist only in terms of how you relate to her. You do or do not meet her needs. You do not have an independent existence. That was a tough thing to grow up with. I did not grow up in a traditional emotional climate. It was a very destructive environment.

"My mother was jealous of me and of my father's affection for me. She was very open about that and very vocal about that. She considered me useless, worthless. Her favorite expression to me was, 'You're a lazy good-for-nothing. All you want to do is sit and read a book all day.' She said it about forty-eight times a week. And I was 'selfish and stubborn and independent,' and all of that was said in a punitive way. I don't remember ever having any support or nurturance or caring. My

parents never touched me unless they hit me. I don't remember ever being hugged. I don't remember ever being comforted,
unless I was sick."

I asked about physical abuse from her mother. Naomi said
that her mother would slap her, but that her father was the one
who would really hit her. It was, as she says, "an ironic twist."

"My father beat the living shit out of me about twice, until I
was black-eyed and bloody nosed, dizzy and generally bruised.
And obviously both times were violent explosions of temper
stemming from his frustration. They had nothing to do with
me except that I happened to be the precipitant. And, in fact,
my mother intervened. On at least one of those occasions, she
was frightened he was really going to hurt me." Naomi was
silent for a while. "No, it wasn't physical abuse that was my
problem. It was emotional abuse. I was emotionally hacked up,
consistently, constantly.

"I know I told one of my therapists that the first thing I had
to do was burrow my way out of an emotional pile of shit
eighty stories deep before I could see the light. I feel that I have
had to dig my way out to be able to learn how to live. And I
was thirty-five before I did it. I don't know where it came from,
that drive to make it out of that pile of shit."

I said that I think it is our nature to seek that light, and she
agreed, absolutely. She mentioned that in her teaching of psychology, she is very much in accord with the theories of Adler
and Maslow who describe a positive striving in human beings.
But she remembers, too, that Maslow also said that a striving
toward health is dependent on other basic needs having been
met. First you have to survive, then you have to have some
feeling of safety to build on.

Obviously, Naomi has looked closely at the sources of her
motivation for choosing not to have children. "It is very clear
to me that much of it comes from my mother. My conscious
conviction, ever since I can remember, was that I was never
going to have a life like hers. I didn't like her, to begin with,

was earning more money than my father and would always earn more money than my father, that it didn't have to be that way. And the men I went to college with were earning four times as much as I did the minute they graduated from college. But somehow I always knew I would have to take care of myself, that I really couldn't trust anybody else to do that."

I expressed amazement that she went to college at all and asked if it had been supported by her family.

"Yes and no. And it is not amazing at all that I went, because that was my route out. I could focus on it. I told my fifth grade teacher that I was going to college and she was the first person who didn't laugh, bless her soul. That was my most single-minded goal from then on.

"No, I was not supported by my father. I had the most vicious fight of our entire lives when I came home from the eighth grade and announced that when I went to high school I was going to take the college prep course. He blew up and hollered and screamed and said why didn't I be sensible and go into a business course and be a secretary so I could get a good job and support myself. Both of us being stubborn, he ended up saying he would never give me a penny and I said I would never take a penny of his damn money.

"One time, while I was still in college, I had quite a lot of money and my father needed some, so he borrowed it from me. Then he kept sending me money while I was at college and I kept deducting it from the amount he owed me. When I went home one time at Christmas, he said something about how much he owed me, and I said no, he only owed me such and such. I showed him how I had been deducting everything he had sent me. He wept, because he'd been involved in sending me money and not in paying me back. It was a bitter issue with us.

"My mother, on the other hand, did help in this way: she let me keep all the money that I earned." After her father left, Naomi worked every summer and part time after school. When she went away to college in 1952, she had fifteen hun-

but even more important, her life was just terribl
work, it was dull, brutal. I always had an awarene
ents' sexual relationship, because we always lived
little house with no privacy and thin walls. I wa
their sexual relationship was painful and brutal a

"My mother didn't have any decent clothes, sl
ways have something that somebody gave to her t
over and it wouldn't fit and it looked awful. Her lif
there was nothing in it that was interesting or excit
ant or rewarding or easy. I wasn't going to live that
it in my bones. Obviously, inevitably, I associated
way with being married and having children. I dc
ever made a conscious decision not to marry and hav
It was years before I recognized that as a decision. (
was an unconscious decision that occurred during m
But I know that vision of my mother and her life wa
important single factor in my decision. It was miser

"I remember when my father got out of the army v
eleven or twelve. He got a lot of money, his musterin
I guess. We made this big trip into town and, oh Go
my mother two dresses and a coat, and that's the fi
remember her having something that was new.

"I remember one time I was with this guy I was
marry and we were walking down the street in Bosto
walked by a piano store. I took lessons, somehow, whe
kid, and I had always wanted a piano. I said, 'Oh, I'd re
to have a piano,' and he said when we got married he'
one. I remember being so astonished that I couldn't c
that information. Whew! Nobody buys you things just
you want them and love them. It just didn't seem po

Her idea of marriage was one of privation, and she
down so badly in that part of her thinking that she did
get as far as thinking about children. "If you got marr
were stuck with this awful life. On a more rational leve
pose it occurred to me, once I had gotten through coll

dred dollars. A full tuition scholarship, and a room and board scholarship from her high school enabled her to use the money for clothes, books, and travel. "In the culture I came from, if you started earning money, you paid room and board at home, and my mother's relatives gave her a hard time because she didn't force me to pay room and board when I was fourteen. In that sense she enabled me to save a reasonable amount of money that I would otherwise not have been able to save. And she supported me by being pleased and proud that I was going to college."

There was a long pause. I commented that she seemed pretty comfortable with the choices she had made.

"I am, but I still feel a loss in not having a close relationship with a man. I've never had a satisfying relationship with a man that lasted for more than a few months. There is a richness and growth which that experience involves that I just haven't had, and probably never will have. I'm not very optimistic about that. In a funny sort of way, the older I get, the less possible it seems. The more clearly my own personality is formed and defined, the less compromise I'm willing to make. On the other hand, the more secure I am, the more open I am. The more flexible I think I could be, the more possible a really caring relationship becomes.

"I can't be that optimistic about it, though, and I do see that as a real loss. But the difference is that now I see it as a loss, and for many years, I saw it as a failure. The difference in that perception came after my first experience with the women's movement."

She told about going to a conference on women and higher education, a federally-funded event for thirty-five people. Thirty-two of the people attending were women. Most of them were administrators or professors, many with Ph.D.'s. Pretty intimidating. Naomi realized that she was "the only woman over twenty-six, who was not a nun, who had never been married." And that was even more intimidating.

"So I had a little difficulty the first few days, but it was interesting because within about five days, as I got to know these women, they began to seek me out. That really blew my mind. In varying ways, they all said, 'I really respect your decision. If it would ever have occurred to me that I could have lived my life alone, I would never have married that . . . whatever, drunk, son-of-a-bitch, lovely but weak, etc., man.' By the time the two-week conference was over at least half the women had in some way or another expressed that to me. That was the first time I had ever been respected for being single. I was thirty-seven. That was such an affirming thing, I can't tell you. I was high for . . . for years!"

But she told me the other side of it. "I knew a number of men in college who were really good guys. I unconsciously protected myself in a lot of ways. I never permitted myself to get close enough to any of the really good ones to be tempted to make any kind of decision at a conscious level. I protected myself by only getting involved with son-of-a-bitches. It wasn't such a big loss, because you were really better off without 'em."

I asked her about the man she had once thought of marrying. She described him as "lovely, but so scared." And he bore the burden of his family's great expectations. "At twenty-one, he already had an ulcer."

She continued, "He was wonderful for me, though, because he was the first person, apart from my sister, who convinced me that he really did love me. I had never been able to feel loved. But he was the one who broke off that relationship. I've asked myself a number of times, if I would have had the courage not to marry him if he hadn't broken up with me? I'm not really sure. Who knows?

"I have been eternally grateful to him though, because it would have been a disaster. He was a very traditional, loving, smothering chauvinist. Had we married, I would have either had children and been a crazy, neurotic, child-abusing wife, or we would have divorced. I'm sure that my growth would have been compromised, perhaps beyond all survival. I'm not sure I ever would have emerged with any sort of clarity."

Naomi told me that her parents have not put any pressure on her to marry and have children. "That's interesting to me, because I've thought about how it might have been different if I'd come from a family where that was considered important. Not only has there been no pressure on me, but, like I said about my mother, she really has no concept of anyone's existence beyond her own. My father and I have what formerly was called an Oedipus fixation in our relationship. There's always been a lot of ambiguity and seductiveness—Daddy's little girl stuff—between us that it has taken me a long time to get over, if I have gotten over it. There was a covert message that I wasn't supposed to grow up, be my own person, or be anyone else's woman."

Recently, however, her father had a bad accident and had to turn to his two daughters for help. It has meant a difficult, but significant, change in their relationship.

"My father has expressed his feelings about my life. He said to me recently, 'Clearly you're much better off than your sister.'" Her sister married, had a child, and went through a difficult marriage and a painful divorce. "So he has acknowledged his approval of my choices in some way, I suppose.

Regrets?

"I'm a Gemini and ambivalence is our middle name. I told someone a few years ago that one of the few things in my life about which I didn't have any ambivalence was that I didn't have any children. And then I thought about it some more (she laughs) and I thought, I am not sorry that I didn't have children. But there is something I'm sorry about, and that is that I didn't have the kind of life which would have enabled me to have children in the way I would like to have children.

"Given the life I was, there is no way that I could have had or wanted anyone being dependent on me—I mean it took me until I was thirty-seven to grow up myself. It took all the time and all the energy and all the money I could muster. There was simply no way that I could have shared that, constructively, with a poor, God-loving little child. A child would have been very deprived, had I been its mother."

But there's just a bit of ambivalence even so. Naomi described a visit to a doctor when she was around forty to discuss a reliable alternative to the birth control pills she could no longer safely take. The doctor suggested that, if she really didn't want to have children, the obvious choice was to have her tubes tied.

"I remember looking at him like he'd just told me to jump off the twenty-fifth floor. I literally pushed my chair away from his desk and moved myself about two feet away from him."

Neither of us said anything for a long while after that.

Finally Naomi said, "I am a role model for many people, as a teacher and as a feminist, and one of the things that worries me about what I've said is that someone will see some kind of wisdom in all this that isn't there. I made my decisions, many of them certainly neurotic, because of my own circumstances. And I had some sexual hangups. I was a virgin until I was twenty-five. Sheer terror was a lot of the reason I didn't marry. I also had low self-esteem and I was self-destructive. I couldn't believe that anyone could love me, and luckily I didn't form real attachments with any of the crazy people I had relationships with. Thank God I never got pregnant.

"I remember one of my cousins saying one time, when I was around fourteen, 'You're never going to marry anyone unless it's really right.' She saw that in me even then."

I asked Naomi if she encounters either prejudice or envy in regard to her childlessness.

"Yes I do, both. A few years ago, I took a semester off and went to Nepal and India. People expressed a lot of envy. I heard it from both men and women. They said, 'You're able to make that kind of choice.'

"Prejudice. Thousands of people have asked me, 'Why isn't

a lovely girl like you married?' If I hear that one more time, I'll scream. My pet peeve is when people, especially men, say to me, 'After all, you don't have any responsibilities.' I get so angry. There is no one to back me up if something happens. I have felt envy of people with two incomes—they have a security I never can have."

We could have talked all night, but it was getting very late and I had to work the next day. The rain was still coming down in buckets, and I had a long drive ahead of me. Naomi's story, though it had been full of courage and hope, had still left me sad. Sad that she has not yet found a man with whom it can be "really right." And a little afraid, as she is, that maybe she never will. It is so easy to say, after you have met him, "Oh yes, I knew that if I just waited long enough and didn't settle for someone who wasn't really right, he would come along and we would recognize each other, oh yes."

I've said it myself. But I didn't always believe it. And it doesn't always happen that way.

12

Sal

I'll Probably Regret It

SAL GREW UP POOR, had a baby and gave it up for adoption, got pregnant again, had an abortion, got married, divorced, and now is living with a man in a strong and caring relationship. That's a lot of living in thirty-six years, and a lot of hurt. But she's still searching and growing, as courageous as ever.

I met Sal several years ago; although we both sensed a kindred spirit between us, we didn't really get to know each other. As she says, "I'm a very private person." The Sal I knew was a very intelligent, sensitive, and young-looking thirty-six year old woman who was frustrated by feeling stuck in a job and work environment that suited neither her abilities nor her temperament. She readily agreed to an interview, to my surprise and delight.

I drove up to Sal's house in the mountain foothills for dinner. It was spring, but the snow was several feet deep in the hills, and we walked over the crumbling crust of it up to a high ridge to watch the sunset before dinner.

Sal shares her house with Joe, who has been part of her life for four years. They served me a fine dinner and then our conversation began. Because Sal's partner is only minimally a part of her decision not to have children, and because he has a child who is with his former wife, my conversation was primarily with Sal. Joe joined us once in a while, but usually just to ask questions.

Sal's face changed as she talked. Sometimes, her eyes would cloud over with unshed tears; sometimes her face relaxed serenely. I think it was a relief for her to tell her whole story.

"I guess a lot of the way I am was shaped by the fact that I came from a poor family. And I didn't have a very happy childhood, although in a lot of ways it was probably better than a lot of people's childhoods.

"I was in a weird position because I was poor, but intellectually ahead of most of the people I dealt with. And I always felt . . . different. I didn't know how to deal with people. I think I was always afraid of people. I didn't know how to respond to them. And because I was afraid of people, my defense was to think of myself as being intellectually superior. It gave me an out. It would have been too painful to really look at why I felt different, so I simply felt superior because I got better marks.

"My father is a very quiet, very shy person. He hardly ever talks. He doesn't even talk to his own family. My mother is very talkative. She's very outgoing. I've always felt kind of sorry for her because she's always lived in a situation in which she hasn't had any social life.

"My parents were always poor and they never had much to do with other people. When you think of poor people, you think of a lot of conviviality, a lot of getting together on Saturday and having a good time. My parents never did that. They always kept to themselves. My father doesn't like people very much and that was reflected in our never going anywhere. We hardly ever went to see anybody.

"I have a sister who is three years older and I have two brothers who are really a sort of second family. My brother Richard was born when I was sixteen. In a lot of ways I feel like his mother. I took a lot of the burden of his existence upon myself. I was living at home and took care of him for all those years. I used to read to him every night. I changed his diapers and fed him. He was like my child. I've often wondered what would have happened if I hadn't had Richard as a younger brother. Maybe he satisfied a lot of my maternal instincts.

"I left home when I was nineteen. I started college, but I was really overwhelmed by the number of people there. I lacked identity and had no sense of direction. I was going to college because people said I should. I thought that I could stay at home and read and get the same thing. I was homesick, I felt out of place, I didn't have any money. So I went home and I stayed there for a year. I felt like a failure and when anyone asked what I was going to do with the rest of my life, I felt really threatened."

After a year at home, Sal left again and got a job and began meeting people. She lived with several other single women and began going out with men for the first time in her life. But she was not thinking of marriage, or motherhood. "I never had dreams of becoming a mother. I had played with dolls, and I liked little kids, but . . .

"The first guy I went out with was sort of an intellectual. We used to write poetry to each other. He was my first, real male romance. When I turned twenty, he sent me one red rose and bought me champagne which I thought was the ultimate in romance.

"But when I was twenty I met another guy and that's when I lost my virginity. I think the only reason I didn't get pregnant then was because he was sterile.

"Another man got me pregnant when I was twenty-four. He didn't want to marry me; he was still in school. So I had an illegitimate child and gave it up for adoption. I didn't want to keep it. That was twelve years ago and women didn't keep their illegitimate children. I like to think I wanted to do what was best for the child. But now I really think I was trying to do what was best for me, which was to get out of it with a minimum of pain and discomfort. But it was still pretty painful. Now I can go for days at a time without thinking about it.

"If he had offered to marry me, I might have been dumb enough to accept, but he sort of abandoned me after he found out I was pregnant. He did try to get me an abortion. We went to New York but it didn't work out. I felt so alone.

"When the baby was born, the hospital staff tried to keep some semblance of normality. They had us go and feed the babies, which was really terrible. I was introduced to motherhood and then it was all torn away from me.

"It still hurts a lot. I think about it. Somewhere there's a twelve year old girl running around and she's my daughter and I don't know who she is, or what she's going to grow up to be. I kind of wonder if she's having a happy childhood."

Sal assured me that her decision at that time to give up her baby was not a decision that she never wanted children. She was mostly concerned about how people would react if she kept it. "I've always had a horror of what people would think of me." Her father still does not know about it. Her mother was very supportive; she had married because she had been pregnant.

"Strangely enough, I didn't get bitter about men. I didn't even feel bitter about the father. After everything was over, he came back and even wanted to marry me. But it was too late then. He was very upset when I told him to go away. I guess I figured that it could have happened to anyone and I was just unlucky.

"I hadn't been using any kind of birth control. I figured it would never happen. But when it did it was awful. I thought if I could just live through that, nothing would ever bother me again. I know that's not true, but I remember thinking that I would never want anything again except to be normal.

"It's such an indignity. There are all these things happening to you that you can't do anything about. Not being able to sleep at night. And then the actual process of birth. I went through all the bad parts, all the pain, but I couldn't have any of the rewards."

When it was all over, Sal went back to work at the same place, with the same people. They all knew that she had been pregnant. But she didn't say anything and neither did they, and after a while things were fairly comfortable. Several years passed.

"I got pregnant again. But I was a little smarter this time. I had an abortion. It was kind of scary. That was before abortions were legal here. The guy I was seeing at the time arranged the whole thing. I just knew that anything would be better than going through what I had gone through before.

"It didn't do anything to me physically. It was just kind of . . . ugly. And I was alone again. I drove down and back the same day and I was really tired. The guy didn't volunteer to go and I guess I didn't really want him to. I asked a friend of mine to go, but she was really upset and was afraid something would happen to me. She tried to talk me out of it, but I was at the point where I would rather have something terrible happen to me than go through a birth and adoption again. And I didn't want to have the baby and keep it. I couldn't handle it financially or any other way. I wasn't going to do it without support.

"I guess I always thought that if I did get married I would have children. But when I got married, I was twenty-eight and I didn't want to have children right away. And then I thought that if I did have children, I'd have to keep working and what's the point of having kids if you just have to leave them with some babysitter all the time?

"When we first got married, my husband wasn't making much money. If we had decided to have a child, I would have had to keep working. I didn't want that. And then by the time I got around to thinking it might be nice to have a child, things weren't very good between my husband and me.

"There wasn't a point at which I decided not to have children. It just never worked out. I don't think I ever wanted them enough. I thought of what a responsibility it would be if I had children, and I didn't want that responsibility. I thought about the kind of childhood I'd had, and I didn't want to put them through that.

"My husband didn't say that he didn't want children, but he didn't actively want them. If he had, then I might have had a child.

"When I first started living with Joe, I wanted to have his child. I think . . . I think he loved me more than any other person ever had. And I think it would be very nice to have a child under those circumstances. But it just didn't work out. We still don't have much money, and now I'm too old. We talked about it a little when we first started living together, but Joe did not want to have more children. He'd already had a child and that was enough for him.

"It feels like a loss to me, but I don't think I was ever willing to accept the responsibility of having a child. I think part of every woman wants to have a child.

"I'll probably regret it when I get older. I suppose every person wants to leave something of herself, or himself. But even now, when I think about having children, it's probably for the wrong reasons.

"It would be kind of nice to have a child that you could leave with some of your feelings about life and how things should be. Maybe they would carry on your philosophy. Which is kind of dumb, because they are not going to do that.

"It would be nice to have a friend. I think that must be one of the nicest parts of parenthood, when your child gets older and is your friend, a special kind of friend.

"And then there's that thing about babies being so cute and cuddly. They're like kittens, they grow up and then they're not cute and cuddly any more. I think I do have a maternal instinct but it gets expressed in weird ways like babying my dog. He's sort of a child substitute.

"I think part of the reason I never had a child to keep was because I had two brothers. They were like my own children and I took on a lot of the responsibility of parenting. I still feel responsible in a certain way. I used to feel so close to Richard. I felt that I would never get married if it would make him unhappy.

"My family never put any pressure on me to have children. I think they'd like to have grandchildren. They have only one. But it might be a relief to them that I am childless, too. If I'd had children, I might not have been able to have helped them financially.

"I feel very sorry for people who have had children—who have had a lot of children—without wanting them. Women who don't really want them, but are stuck with them because society says they should have children.

"I don't feel sorry for people who want to have children and can't. It's really easy to have kids if you want to adopt children. And if you aren't willing to adopt, then you probably don't want them enough.

"I guess the main thing I feel is left out. It's one of those things that you have to do to be accepted, like getting married. It's sort of a badge of maturity. You're not really considered mature unless you've raised a child. Any idiot can have and raise a child. You don't have to do a particularly good job. But it is just another aspect of American life. Maybe just life in general. People don't think you have come into your own, don't know what it's all about, unless you've raised a child. I've been through a lot and I think I'm probably as mature as most people. But I'll probably never be accepted as that."

We talked a bit about purpose in life. So many people seem to feel that their main purpose in life is to have children. Sal said, "I don't think having children gives you more purpose in life. As long as there is something to look forward to, there's a purpose. Maybe the purpose is to be the kind of person you are, to affirm your own existence. Maybe I'm here just because

I'm different. There are people who live just because of their children. I think most people have children for the wrong reasons.

"I guess that I saw my parents in a not particularly happy relationship. They got married because my mother was pregnant, and all these years they've stayed together because of that one thing—even though the baby died three months after it was born.

"It would be nice to have a child to read to, to share all the stories that were my favorites when I was a kid. It would be good to share all the good times I've had. A large part of the reason I never had children was that I never thought I could afford children. I guess if you want them badly enough, that doesn't stand in your way. But I think about all the things I never had when I was a kid.

"I guess if people want children they go ahead and have them without thinking about how they are going to be raised. I think that is irresponsible and I couldn't do that.

"Another reason I didn't have children when I was married was that I was afraid my husband wouldn't accept his share of the responsibility for them. He wouldn't even accept his share of the responsibility for doing housework. I believe that people should be married a couple of years before having children, and by the time we had been married two years, it had become apparent to me that there was something wrong with the marriage.

"I'd like to work with children, but I don't know if it is to make up for not having them. I just like children. I enjoy them. Sometimes I feel like I'm missing a lot. I think it will get harder as I get older. So many people have children and that will make me just that much more different. I probably will regret it.

"But I think the time to have children is when you are young—before you are thirty. It takes a lot of time and energy to care for children. It would have been very difficult for me because I am a very private person and I need lots of time to myself. I think I was lucky because I was never subjected to a lot of pressure to have children, either from my family or my husband.

"Things just didn't work out for me to have children. But if I had really wanted them enough, I would have had them."

I asked Sal if there was one last thing she would like to add and she said yes. "This has not gone at all the way I thought it would. I was going to give you a really strong statement on why I don't believe in having children. It didn't come out that way at all. I guess what you think and what you feel are two different things. You can make some grand intellectual statement, but it doesn't show how you are feeling."

13

Joan

Growing Up Catholic

COMING FROM A LARGE, traditional Catholic family does not exactly guarantee that you will marry someday and have children of your own, but there certainly is a lot of push in that direction. Catholicism's official word still prohibits birth control, abortion, and, heaven forbid, sex for pleasure. But more and more Catholics are making some of these decisions for themselves. For many, that means the end of being a practicing Catholic. Which comes first is often difficult to tell.

Joan came from just such a large, traditional Catholic family; she has decided not to have children. Although she is only twenty-eight, her decision is firm.

"When I was younger," she said, "I always had my brothers and sisters around, and it was always just assumed that we would all have big families. And when we talked with our little friends, we all talked about how many kids we wanted. I wanted all girls. But everyone talked about having kids—that was the way we were brought up. All you talked about was the kind of man you were going to marry and the kind of kids you were going to have."

When Joan was a teenager, her parents began taking in foster children who needed temporary care until other homes could be found for them. All the children in the household were expected to help take care of the foster kids. Joan feels as if she already has had the experience of having children. She certainly knows what is involved in taking care of them. She also resented spending so much of her time and energy taking care of children.

It was during this time that she decided she wanted to be a social worker and work with children. "I switched from actually wanting the kids to working with them."

Joan's adolescence was not exactly a normal one, she says. Having the foster children around was only part of it. "I came from a really strict Catholic family. My older sister was a nun, she was in a convent. Another sister was an honor student at a Catholic high school, and my brother was always a good student, too. But I was always getting into trouble, always skipping school, fighting with my mother. My mother and I never got along. There was so much turmoil. My family was very conservative, had a lot of prejudices, and I began to question that. I was the first one who started stepping out of line. I ran away a lot."

As Joan grew up, her conflicts with her mother worsened, but they had clashed even when she was quite small. "I refused to wear skirts. I was a defiant woman then, too."

High school was a difficult time. Joan started hanging around with people her mother didn't like, opposed her mother's demand that she take over most of the cooking, and got into minor trouble at school. After graduation she moved out of her parents' house, rented an apartment with a friend, and became involved in liberal politics. She was able to be herself, find out what she really thought, and express her differences with her family. "I think that was when, more than any other time, I began to change and to think about kids. Not only personally, but politically in the world. I went beyond thinking it would be terrific to have some little girls.

"I guess over the past few years, working within the

women's movement, I have come to see that I have made a firm commitment not to have kids. Partly, I just don't want the responsibility. I don't want the responsibility of someone else's life on me. I think kids are nice, I really love kids, but I don't want to have any.

"The world isn't stable enough to bring kids into it. There are plenty of kids available if I decide I want to take care of some kids." We were talking at the time when the "Boat People," thousands of homeless Vietnamese refugees, were in the news. "What the hell is going to happen to them? That's part of the political reason I don't want children. I feel I can make as many statements as I want to a child and bring that child up in the lifestyle in which I want to live, but the child still has to deal with the world. And if my lifestyle is so different from the rest of the world, that kid is going to have so many conflicts. But they have to relate sooner or later to some lifestyle, either mine or what's out there. The kid has to go to school and if he or she goes to public school, especially, there are too many influences around that I think would cause a lot of conflict."

Joan had mentioned different lifestyles. I asked her to talk about that a little more. She hesitated, then told me there was something she did not know how to say. She assured me that it had nothing to do with her decision, which was made before, but that it did have a lot to do with her lifestyle. She didn't want it in the book. I assured her that I would disguise the details of her life so that her identity would not be known; if she read the interview and gave her okay, I would use it. Otherwise this part would be omitted.

"I'm a lesbian. Some of my family members know, and some don't. How it would influence my job would be another story. I want it to be clear that this is not the reason I decided not to have children. I feel that they are separate issues, even though I have been a lesbian since before I made the decision not to have kids."

Joan and her partner have been together quite a while now.

Her partner wants to have children. Joan doesn't. They don't know how they will resolve this difference, which does not lend itself to compromise. Joan does not want to impose her politics and her lifestyle on a child. She knows that some people do it and it seems to work out all right, but she doesn't want to risk it. She also fears that a child might react so strongly to her unconventional lifestyle that the child would become super-conventional. That would be hard—seeing your child become what you rebelled against.

"The women's movement means everything to me. I have practically everything invested in it, in one way or another. Women are very important to me in terms of support. It was with women that I began to understand who I was and to relate to myself and other people. Until I got involved with the women's movement, I modeled myself after my father. There was this very stoic person, you never knew how he felt; he was tense and tight, and I thought that was the way to be.

"He used to say things like, 'You can't trust anybody. Just watch out for yourself, don't expect anyone to pat you on the back.' That's the way I grew up. I never talked to anyone about my feelings and they were always held inside of me. I spent a lot of energy pretending I didn't have them, and becoming tight and rigid, just like my father."

In 1971, Joan became involved in the women's movement. For the first time in her life, she felt that someone understood what she was going through. "Specifically *women*—we could relate beyond just our politics. We could sit and talk and go through everything in our lives and have some connection.

"I remember when I was young, listening to songs on the radio, thinking they were always about women crying over losing their men. I could never understand why that was the only type of song on the radio. I said to my sister, 'How come everyone is crying about love?' And she said, 'That's all there is.' And I thought, 'No, there's got to be more.'

"I was really close to my little brother for many years, important years in my life, when we shared things. I remember worrying about when he got married, whether his wife would be closer to him than I was. And so we made this pact not to get married, which I'm sure he's forgotten about, although he isn't married.

"I guess I was always daring because I had brothers around. I was always playing sports and doing things. I was a tomboy. I just read somewhere, I think in *Notes of a Feminist Therapist*, what it takes to make a strong, aggressive woman: a tomboy, because they are willing to take risks."

Both men and women have innate abilities, but women have been taught to disown some of those abilities, especially ones that require strength or mechanical skill. "We had to stop and put the chains on our tires last night, and I didn't know how to do it. I felt really stupid, because here I am this great feminist talking about how women should take control of their lives, and I can't even put chains on my car. But my partner said, 'Of course not, no one ever would have taught you.' It's one of the earliest forms of discrimination."

I asked Joan again what the political motive was for her decision, since being a lesbian is not equatable with deciding not to have children. "People might automatically assume I don't want children because I am a lesbian. I just feel that my responsibilities, if I have any at all, are to myself and to effecting changes in my immediate circle of life, if I can. It's not a great world, and I don't trust it a lot. In order for me to bring a child into this world, I'd have to feel really good about where things were at. Not only in my little life but in the whole world, and the world is so crazy. It just doesn't seem to be a safe place to bring people into."

Nuclear power, air pollution, and corrupt governments are just some of the things that make the world feel unsafe. Joan also feels that women have been conditioned to have children and that they have not been told fairly about some of the bad aspects of being mothers.

"I was talking to a friend of mine, telling her I was going to be interviewed for this book. She is divorced and has custody of four kids and she's going nuts. She has nobody . . . I mean, she has friends, but most people don't get into doing surrogate parenting. So she's got the burden of all those kids. She said that anyone who thinks they want to have a kid should try it out first by taking care of one for a while. It's not easy.

"But nobody tells you how hard it gets. It's not just a few years, it's for the rest of your life. You always have some connection, whether or not you get along or even see each other.

"There's this whole myth about this wonderful new baby—you'll feel like a real woman if you have a kid. But then you are a mother, you're no longer considered a woman. It's a very sudden switch. That was your goal and now you have met it and you are stuck. I remember seeing a woman on a talk show years ago. She said, 'I'm not a woman, I'm a mother.' Everyone started cheering."

I asked Joan if her mother had tried to influence her to have children.

"Yeah, at different points she would say she hoped she would have lots of grandchildren, that her goal was to see us all marry and have children—as long as we married someone of our own race. And my parents are Catholic, and birth control is not allowed, and they really bought it. They both came from relatively big families, too. So there was just this whole undertone of having children, and not only having children to please your mother, but to make her a grandmother and keep the whole cycle going. But that was back when I was fourteen or fifteen.

"If you don't want children people say you are too self-centered and you don't think about anybody but yourself and your own needs. But if you can't think about your own needs, you can't deal with somebody else's. You have to know yourself pretty well before you can say, 'Okay, I know I can give a part of my life to someone now.' Especially someone who is going to depend on you for so long.

"I don't think very many people are able to acknowledge their own needs and allow that to stand for itself. We're so conditioned to think we are just here to create people after us, instead of living a nice life and taking care of other people, not necessarily children.

"I guess that another reason I don't want kids is that I want total control over my life—at least I want to eliminate as many external influences as I possibly can, the ones which limit what I can do for myself. I want to make decisions, not have them made for me.

"One of the things I get really upset about, and it is probably because of the type of family I grew up in, is people who have kids and don't have the patience for them, who really resent them because they have to be there all the time. And then my sister, who has two kids, is really smart, but she has done nothing since she got married except stay home and have two kids.

"When someone has a kid, everyone talks about how much they will enjoy it, but no one gives the mother a chance to say, 'I'm exhausted, this is terrible sometimes.' Everyone goes into this whole myth that it is going to be fun from the time the kid is born. People need to know more about what they are getting into, that sometimes it is going to be boring drudgery, in addition to the nice parts. I saw a lot of that when I was younger, and I am totally convinced that that has much to do with my decision not to have kids. Some of it was nice, having all those kids around, but I got to see both sides of it."

Joan's mother worked from the time Joan was about ten. Her father worked at a job that was just for money, with no satisfaction. "My family didn't take many risks. With so many kids, they probably couldn't. And they were just not the sort of people to take risks. They don't like to be different. My mother says, 'Other people go along with their lives even if they are unhappy, why can't you do that?' "

As Joan has matured, she has seen that her parents did the best they could, and that life was not easy for them. She is willing to take responsibility for her own life. We talked a little about no longer needing our parents, either for approval or for love, even though it is nice to have both. And we both said that we could see how hard it would be to let go of children after having taken care of them and seen them grow for twenty years.

Joan said, "I guess I am being a little self-protective when I don't want to have kids, because I don't want to be rejected at some point. Have my values rejected, have the kid say 'goodbye,' 'thank you,' or 'no thank you.' It must be hard not to have people there who have always been there."

I again asked Joan if there wasn't more to the political side of her decision. She seemed to talk more about personal influences.

"I suppose there is more to it, but I have not really taken the time to sit down and separate the political from the personal. They are so entwined."

I told her that it seemed to me that to have a child is almost to capitulate to conditioning, or appear to, and something in her resists that. I said it because I have often felt that way. I have resisted doing what everyone else does, just because everyone else is doing it. Often, I really disagree with what the crowd is doing, but sometimes I am just trying to be different. Joan said it might be that way for her, too.

"My life as it's been in the past ten years, all equals—no children. There are different points in my life where I have thought about not having children, and now they all just connect. Maybe I was around twelve when I first realized there was more to life than kids, and it comes back all the time. So each time reinforces the other. There are political things behind that, but also the feeling that my life would be halted if I had a kid."

I asked her, "Being the sort of person you are, feeling the

way you do about parenting, it might mean that other things would have to take second place?"

"Yes, and I guess I don't want that to happen. My need to do things is more global than the immediate experience of having a child. I don't feel a need to have the experience of physically having a child.

"I guess if when I get older I feel like it was a mistake not to have children, I can adopt a child. The old age thing—having kids just to make sure you'll be taken care of when you are old—doesn't make any sense to me. I figure that I will always have a support system of friends, people who care about me and I about them, and we will take care of each other. I also think it would help if people would stop looking at kids as a way of taking care of their own needs. I see taking care of my own needs as one of the things I am supposed to do in life."

Children have been an important part of Joan's personal and professional life. "I have found a lot of fulfillment through other people's kids."

I asked her how other people, those outside her close relationships, have reacted to her decision not to have children.

"People's first reaction is surprise that I would say that; then their tendency is to say, 'That's because you haven't found anybody yet,' which used to make me mad, because it sounded like it was negating what I was saying. But I tell people why, and they understand my reasons, which is nice. All the people I went to high school with have kids. But a lot of people say to me that if they had *thought* about having kids, they wouldn't have done it.

"I'm astounded when I ask people how they went about making the decision to have a kid. How much thought did they give to how they would work out any major differences they might have about raising a kid? I asked my sister if she and her husband talked about raising kids before they had any, and she said, 'No, we just had them. Why do you have to talk about it?' "

We talked a little more about our sadness and anger that most women who have had children did not know that they had a choice. For some women, having children is wonderful. For others, it is miserable. Until recently, there have been few acceptable role models for other ways of life. Unmarried women were old maids; unmarried men were bachelors.

Joan remembers watching a television show when she was in high school. "They asked Sal Mineo how he was able to avoid being trapped—meaning marriage. They asked a woman, 'Why isn't a beautiful thing like you married?' It drove me just bananas."

Joan has high hopes for women and for the good influence women will have on the world when they can and do make choices instead of being pushed into roles. For her, this is the revolution.

14

Amanda

Reflections at Eighty-Eight

AMANDA HAD GIVEN me good directions for finding her home in the country. I knew she had been a physician and thought perhaps I would find an elegant older woman surrounded by silver and crystal. I was afraid I would feel uncomfortable in such a setting.

My fantasy, or preconception, proved to be almost totally inaccurate. The only word I could salvage from it was elegant, in the best sense of the word. I found Amanda to be warm, receptive, good-humored, and interested in everything.

Her house was an old farmhouse, well-kept but not pretentiously so. I was delighted to find a fairly late model middle-sized American car in the dirt driveway. Usually American cars don't thrill me much, but this one did because it bespoke a woman in her late eighties who was still getting around in her own automobile.

When the door opened, I was greeted enthusiastically by a smiling woman who immediately made me feel at ease. The house was comfortably but not expensively furnished. Everything, including the dog and cat, looked as if it had been there a long time and felt very much at home. I noticed immediately that almost every wall was hung with a drawing, painting, or watercolor.

153

We sat down in big easy chairs grouped around the fireplace. After asking her permission, I set up the tape recorder—she didn't mind in the least—and we began to talk.

Long before the women's liberation movement, Amanda was a strong, courageous, independent woman who became a doctor after several years as a public health nurse. There was little in her background to predict that then very unusual choice of a profession.

Amanda's family was a very happy one, and "comfortably well off," as she put it. Her father had worked his way up in a small business and done well. He prided himself on being able to provide for his women—Amanda had two sisters—and was dead set against any of them working for a living. But Amanda wanted to be a public health nurse; she had a grandmother in poor health who could have used public health nursing services, but none were available in the area where her farm was located.

Amanda explained, "I wanted to be a nurse way from the beginning and I had books about nursing in my room that I kept under my pillow." Her father would not have liked seeing the books.

The one thing unusual in Amanda's family was that the girls were encouraged to go to college. This was in the early nineteen hundreds. The family believed in education and it didn't matter if you were a man or a woman. Neither of her parents had the opportunity to go to college; they were both determined to provide that chance for their children.

But going to college was not what started Amanda on the road to becoming a doctor. She took the usual liberal arts course, graduated, and returned home to be with her mother after the death of her father. That is how things were done then. "It would have been unthinkable to leave my mother." Her two sisters had married and left home. "I stayed at home for five years, and by that time it was obvious that wasn't my forte," she said, with marvelous tact and humor. "It wasn't a bad life, but it wasn't what I wanted." The old dream of becoming a nurse was pulling on her, and she decided to go to nursing school.

After three years of school and several years of nursing, she practiced public health nursing in a small city which had a very high infant mortality rate. Everyone was working hard to find the cause and reduce the rate of infant deaths, and it did drop dramatically after she arrived. An English nurse and a trained midwife had arrived at about the same time. Amanda laughingly said, "We liked to think we had been responsible for the drop, but I think the pasteurization of milk had a great deal more to do with it."

They all worked very closely with the doctors and attended many home deliveries. "That was probably what started me into medicine, because the doctors urged me to go into medicine."

By then, Amanda was already thirty-five years old. She started medical school much older than any of her classmates; all of them were men. During our conversation, Amanda referred to them always as "the boys."

"They were very helpful. They were also very frank. In our senior year, we were sent out two-by-two to work with different physicians, and the burning question of the day was who was going with me. One of the boys met me on the steps and asked me whom I was going with and I said I didn't know. He told me he wouldn't mind going with me himself if he hadn't promised someone else. He said, 'You've got a car and you could take me 'round.' I told him the car was on its last legs and I didn't know if it would make spring term or not. He looked very serious then and said, 'Don't let that get around, that's your only drawing card.' "

After medical school and an internship, Amanda took one year of post-graduate work which qualified her to become a pediatrician. During the Depression, she started a medical practice which she continued for twenty-five years.

Her practice was a strenuous one, especially during the war years. "You didn't get enough sleep or the right food, as I discovered when an anemic patient came in. I pricked her finger and showed her the color of her blood. She didn't seem convinced, so I told her I would show her a good drop of blood. I pricked my own finger and it was so much worse than hers that it was an eye opener to me.

"So many of the men were away, and you did everything. You had to." But it was a wonderful time to be practicing medicine, she said, "Because of the cooperation and the warm feelings between the doctors. It was also a time of very warm feelings with the patients." There was friendship, mutual confidence.

Amanda had said that her father was very much opposed to her having a profession at all. What about her mother?

"Well, she didn't oppose it as much. She didn't want me to leave, because it left her in the home alone. But all the time I was in medical school I came home often, on weekends. After I came back to practice, she went to medical meetings with me and seemed to enjoy them. And I think she was happy about it afterwards."

I asked if her mother had been at all concerned that she was not married and having children.

"No, no I don't think anybody ever thought about it one way or the other."

Clearly, for most of Amanda's working years, her work was her life. She had a few friends she could drop in on for a late cup of coffee, but mostly she worked, ate, and slept.

I said, "Do you ever look back on your life and think maybe you would have done something differently?"

"No."

I commented that she didn't seem like a person who spent too much time thinking about that.

"No, I don't. I think when you get to be my age you have to make a conscious effort not to. You can't do it. You are living now. You can't have the things that are lost, you have to enjoy what you have now."

I asked, "When you were deciding to become a doctor, did you feel like you were giving anything up?"

"No. Not even art, and I loved to draw. Since I've retired I've had a great deal of pleasure from it. But no, it never competed with medicine. I wanted medicine. I did, sometimes late at night, draw my cat or dog by the fireplace, but I didn't do much of anything with that.

"I enjoyed the things I did. And after I retired, I loved retirement. I love to travel and I love drawing. I had a great many happy years doing that. I had a very good outlet in Tucson, a little shop that sold them for me so they didn't pile up. I had a lot of fun with it."

What about children and family?

"I didn't have time. Of course I worked with children a great deal—I limited my practice to pediatrics after the first ten years. I saw plenty of children."

Did it bother her not to have children of her own?

"No. You can't have everything." Amanda had a friend, also a pediatrician, who married and had children, but gave up her practice while her children were young. That was not something Amanda wanted to do. "I wanted pediatrics." She had a housekeeper just to keep her own household going as it was. She lived alone, often with a dog for companionship, and liked her life. "If I had had to run the house, I couldn't have done it. It was a busy time and a good time."

I told Amanda that it was interesting to me that she took a very different path than most of the people she grew up with. "Yes," she said, "at that time nursing and teaching were the two professions that women went into." Even college was unusual. "I was just reading the story of Dana Hall, and that said it didn't become common for women to go to college until the 1920's. And I went in 1906, of course."

But her college course, "a ladies cultural course," she said, amused, had not prepared her for medical school. She had to take courses in chemistry and other sciences for a year before she could even start medical school. During that year, she also worked half time.

Meanwhile, what were most of her friends doing with their lives? "One of them became a teacher and did not marry. One married and had a family. One became a secretary and did not marry. Another one became a teacher and did not marry. Come to think of it, among my closest friends, I can only think of one who married." She was not sure if that was unusual for that time.

Amanda has stayed in touch with most of those friends, and friends have been very important in her life. "Of course as you grow older and lose members of your family, you are even more dependent on your friends. I'm lucky that I have good friends."

Most of Amanda's young friends are having children, and that is just what they should be doing if they want to, she thinks. "But if you have children, that's it. You don't have the time. That's a full-time job in itself. You can't divide. You choose to have a family, or you choose your profession, and both are important. I think it is very lucky that some people want one and some want the other.

"You have to let kids know they are important. Here, we are a very old-fashioned road, really. The young people are all important in their homes and they know it. Families need to be real families. They need to have a certain quality.

"I think if you want to do something enough, you can do it. But if people are vascillating with something else they want to do, then they have to decide. A young friend of mine is planning what she wants to do when she gets out of college. She doesn't want to have a family and she wants to go into the Peace Corps. But I'm old-fashioned enough to think that almost any woman, if the right man came along, would want to marry. But it depends on that a lot."

I asked her if she might have married if the right man had come along. With no hesitation, she answered, "Oh, I'm sure. The right one never came along. And I was pretty fussy, I guess, because I liked my job. But I enjoyed my life. I wouldn't have changed it."

We visited a bit, about books we were reading, about the news, and then Amanda offered me coffee because I had such a long trip. We went out to the kitchen where she put the pot on to perk, then back to the living room armed with cups of coffee and a plate of Fig Newtons. Then Amanda told me about two things that had happened to her within the past couple of years which really meant a lot to her.

One was that she had been given an award by her college for being a noteworthy alumnus. The other was that she had been voted "Grandmother of the Year" in her state. I asked her how that came about.

"It was a neighbor of mine, I think, who got the idea. It sounded ridiculous to me at first, and everybody laughed when they heard it, but it was very nice. The governor came down and we had a real informal nice party. It was fun."

For about the last eight years, Amanda has been taking care of two young girls whose mother got too sick to care for them. One of those young girls has grown up during that time, married, and had a child. The other is now in college.

"It was a real eye-opener to me. They are really nice girls and they have added a lot to my life. I've learned a lot about young people nowadays, from them. They are kind of old-fashioned—they had a rather strict upbringing, I'm afraid, here with me."

I said that I don't think being strict is necessarily bad. She agreed that sometimes it helps kids know that you take enough interest in them to want certain things done.

I was delighted with the idea that it might be possible to "adopt" a family at almost any point in our lives, if we want to. But Amanda warned me not to count on it, because young people have their own lives to lead and may not want what you do. Amanda also felt that even if you have children, you can't always count on them.

"They may not have the resources. I don't think they should be responsible. Older people live their lives and younger people live theirs. If that is the only reason someone is going to have kids, I would not recommend it."

We talked some more, about writing, about friends, and I told her that I felt I was missing something. I didn't know what to ask her.

Why did she specialize in pediatrics? "Well, I was always interested in that. I think women are more interested in that, generally. I was more interested in that than any other branch of medicine."

Then we talked a bit more about the two girls who came to live with Amanda. "I told them there were two things they had to do. They had to mind me and they had to tell me the truth, and I think they always did. I really had very little trouble with them about going out. I told them I was old and I couldn't sit up waiting for them and I couldn't go to bed if they were out, so they had to come in earlier than most young people. It worked out very well."

I especially noticed, when Amanda was talking about the two girls, that she was delighted that one of them had married happily and was now part of a "thrifty, hard-working couple." About the other girl she said, "She is wonderful with children, and I hope she will work with children." She did not automatically hope that she will *have* children.

We talked about other things, and finally it was time for me to go. I was full of Fig Newtons and coffee and dreading the long drive ahead of me. Amanda stood in her doorway and watched while I backed my car out of the driveway, and I waved to her as I pulled away. She waved back, and I could see her watching the car until it was out of her sight. My mother, too, "watches people away," and now, so do I. The warm glow of kindredness stayed with me for many miles down the road from Amanda's house.

I had not been able to ask some questions, but others had been more than answered.

Conclusion

15

Nonparenthood

The Challenge

SEVERAL YEARS AGO, Ann Landers, an advice columnist, asked her readers to write saying whether they would have children if given the choice again. Of the fifty thousand parents who responded, seventy percent said they felt it wasn't worth it. I don't know how much credibility can be given to that figure, but it indicates a lot of dissatisfaction with parenthood. Possibly much dissatisfaction came from people's not knowing what to expect from parenthood or how to deal with it. Maybe some of those people would not have had children if they had known they had the choice; they might have been better off. And what about their children? Would you like to know your parents felt as those fifty thousand respondents did?

In these pages, you have met men and women who *haven't* had children. Most of them feel good about the choice they made. They have told you something about what it is like to be an adult without children and they have traced how their decisions about parenthood evolved.

Although this book is not intended to be a study of voluntarily childless people in America, I think it worthwhile to identify the patterns of circumstances, reasons, and personalities which emerged in these introspections. This chapter looks at those patterns, and at the risks and the challenge of nonparenthood.

When I started this book, my intention was to talk to possibly fifty couples and individuals in all parts of the country. I wanted to make sure that I met people from many different backgrounds, places, age groups, religious and ethnic groups, and levels of affluence.

Within the limits of my time, money, and methods of finding people to interview, I was able to find a variety of points of view, but I certainly make no claim to have covered all possible reasons for choosing not to have children. At the same time, I am well aware that if I had interviewed even several hundred people, they would still have spoken only for themselves. Their stories would be different in the way that all lives are different.

I chose to do a few stories in depth rather than many at a superficial level. I think that the lives described here show that nonparenthood does not lend itself to simplistic statistical breakdowns.

When we talk about the choice not to have children, only so many considerations are possible. These reasons are limited in number, but each person's life is a new context within which those reasons are uniquely arrived at and assembled. The "how" of people making this decision is almost infinite, but the "why" falls into some identifiable patterns.

I have chosen to group these "whys" into two major categories which are really the two opposite ends of a continuum. Simply stated, these are "Going Toward Something Other than Parenthood," and "Going Away from Parenthood." Most people who don't have children state both reasons for their choice, although a few are distinctly on one side or the other. A word of caution: these categories are only a tool for looking at a mass of information. There are fine lines between ways of expressing reasons for not having children; I'm not suggesting these patterns as the only or best way of characterizing those reasons. One person might say, "I like my life the way it is," and another might say, "I fear that parenthood would change my life for the worse." Those are two different ways of saying essentially the same thing, but what's behind them is different.

Going toward something other than parenthood. Under this heading we find the people who want to do something else with their time, energy, talent, money, or education besides parenting. This something else may be a profession, expression of an artistic talent, a social cause, or a community. After careful consideration of the alternatives, some folks decide that to try to combine parenthood with the other important goals in their lives would be a disservice to both.

Here also are people who are politically and ecologically conscious and conscientious; they choose not to have children as one way of reducing the strain on our burdened ecosystem and social systems. In addition, not having children frees some of their energy for pursuing alternatives to systems that aren't working; some nonparents are educating other people about those alternatives.

A third group could be characterized as people who know themselves well, and on the basis of that knowledge, choose not to have children. They may want to have a lot of peace and quiet, to concentrate on their mate, to stay financially unencumbered. Freedom to travel extensively, to experiment with ways of living, to be spontaneous, may be factors.

Going away from parenthood. Some people see nothing particularly desirable about being a parent. They have little interest in parenthood or may even dislike children or being around children.

Some people go away from parenthood because they do not want to be single parents and they have no partner available to share parenthood. They may want to be parents, but not in their life circumstances.

A few people fear that they would be bad parents because of their own upbringing. People who have been abused as children sometimes feel that they might become abusive parents under stress. They just don't want to take the risk. Or, by the time they feel confident that they could do better, they are too old to have children.

Parenthood involves many unknowns; some people fear those unknowns to the extent that they would rather not have children. They ask: How will parenthood affect me, my relationship with my mate, my whole approach to work, to life? You can't really know until you try; for people who are already happy with their lives, the risk of change may be too great.

Parenthood is also a lot of responsibility of a very special kind: You are responsible for someone else's existence and his or her care and nurturance for many years. Some people do not want that particular kind of responsibility.

Often, people arrive at the same destination by taking vastly different routes, and that's certainly been true here. For some, the road was hard, the journey full of doubt and uncertainty. Others seemed to be following a perfectly marked map they trusted completely. Some didn't know where they were going until they arrived, but there were always a few road marks along the way.

If, for example, you are a woman over thirty-five and you haven't had children and don't currently know a man willing and able to share parenthood with you, you are on the road to remaining without children. And if you aren't inclined to have kids alone, you have practically arrived at that destination.

Many nonparents grew up with the expectation that they would have children, but some didn't give it much thought. Some got married young, some divorced and remarried, some were never married, some are in couples, some are solitary.

Nonparents come from every religious background. Some have professions and some don't, although most are college educated.

If all these people have anything in common, besides not having children, it is that they are thoughtful about their actions and the consequences of those actions. They generally make choices rather than let choices be made for them. And they are able and willing to be different from most of their peers in a substantial and significant way. Most have asked themselves, "What do I really want to do with my life, and can I live with the trade-off that is necessary for me to be able to do that?" They are an introspective lot, these nonparents. They know themselves pretty well as a result. Not all of them have delved deeply into their childlessness, but if anything stands out in my mind after talking to many people without children, this does: self-knowledge.

Having children is like white water canoeing. Once you put that boat in the river and let yourself get swept along by the current, you have no choice but to ride it out. And what you can do to alter the course of the ride is a mixture of skill, knowledge, chance, and the nature of the river. For certain stretches, you are not in control any more. You go with what is there.

Perhaps those who choose to remain childless are not inclined to give up that much control over what happens to them. They *are* willing to take risks. The kind of risk they are willing to take, however, is different. They, too, are traveling down a river which flows of its own accord. If they do not have children and then later regret that loss, they have no control over the past decision which brought them to that regret. They took that risk, and now there is only the present. They may be able to adopt if they are not too old, and if a child is available. But they can never have their own child.

The more I have thought about this, the more I have become aware of the risks of not having children. You risk being different from the majority of your peers, doing something unacceptable and misunderstood. You risk missing a vital human experience and finding out too late that it really mattered to you. You take the risks that any pioneer faces: getting lost, or finding, once you get to where you are going, that it has not been worth the journey.

Being a parent in today's world is most certainly a challenge. Being an adult without children is also a challenge. When you don't have children, your role as an adult is not in any way mapped out. You must find your own way. There is little support for you; few can share with you the task of deciding what to do with a life that is your own. When no one else is depending on you, when material needs are relatively simple and easily met, the challenge is to live a life that has meaning for you.

But why is that a challenge? Wouldn't anyone thrive on the chance to "do whatever he or she wants to do?" I see it as a challenge because having options necessitates having to make decisions, lots of decisions, about your own life. And that's difficult.

If you have children, you can still make decisions about your life, but they *must* involve the needs of your children. If you have children you take a job because you need the money. You decide where to live partly on the basis of the availability of schools. You spend much of your time, energy, and money providing for, teaching, and nurturing your children. Your life has at least one very clear purpose: taking care of your children.

But if you don't have children, you will be without the structure they provide. How you spend your time is completely up to you. What will you do after you get home from work? A whole world in need is out there waiting for you but no one is going to compel you to do anything about it. No one is going to accuse you of neglect or abuse if you ignore those needs completely. Not so if you ignore the needs of your children.

The possibility of serious regret is a real one, especially if you arrive at your middle years and find that you didn't really decide not to have children; you let it happen by default. If you didn't do anything else that felt meaningful and positive for you, you could find yourself saying, "I might as well have had children," or "I feel the loss terribly now."

What about the people who tell you that they once thought they didn't want children, but now that they've had one, they can't imagine life without little Jason or Susie? Well, they have made a decision that seems right for them. People change. Circumstances change. *You* might or might not enjoy being a parent. You are a different person from your friends. You know yourself more fully than anyone else knows you. Even so, the decision is tough. It strains your imagination, awakens your fears, and fosters your fantasies.

So the challenge is to make a choice and then live your chosen life in such a way that you will not have to look back with overwhelming regret. Unfortunately, most of us have not been adequately prepared to make those kinds of choices. Our families, our schools, and our social systems have done little to prepare us; they have sometimes even withheld information, opportunity and support for that kind of decision-making.

I envision several ways to change that. First, I see a society in which every child arrives with this birthright: a child is born after some thoughtful self-assessment, planning, and decision-making on the part of its parents. The child is very much wanted, and the parents have the knowledge, skill, desire, and resources to nurture that child physically and emotionally. ("Parents" could mean people other than the biological parents, I suppose, but I particularly mean the man and the woman who, together, are proposing to create another human being.)

To guarantee such a birthright, we need to do several things. We need to inform young people that having children is a choice—both a personal and a social choice. We need to inform them about the consequences of both parenthood and nonparenthood. We need to give young people a realistic view of what it means to combine careers, relationships, and parenthood, and what the personal, economic and time costs of parenthood are. People deserve the information needed to make thoughtful choices. They also need to be alerted to the way in which advertising, other people, and fictional portrayals of adult life push the message that marriage and children constitute the only normal lifestyle.

We need to treat preparation for possible parenthood with at least as much care as we give to career choices—possibly more. Can we do any less in helping young people make the complex decision of whether to become parents?

Several types of parent training are available; most of them at least raise some of the issues involved in being a good parent. Why not require courses in schools and colleges on how to be a parent, courses that would include emphasis on decision-making about parenthood? These courses would say, "*If* you have children," not "*when.*"

If every child born had been wanted, if every child had parents who knew what was involved in taking care of children, parents who had made a commitment to taking care of their children, we would probably see very little child abuse and neglect. Instead, today, the statistics are very sad. As many as two million children may be abused or neglected each year in the United States, and the numbers seem to be rising.

Second, I see a society in which women are not forced by circumstances to make the choice between motherhood and careers. Men have not had to make that choice because they have had wives who took care of the household and the children. I'm not suggesting a simple role reversal as a solution, unless individual couples find that to be a workable alternative. Just as some women would really rather stay home with the children, some men would really rather stay home while their wives earn the living. There's nothing wrong with that, but it doesn't address the underlying social and economic issues which precipitate such choices.

Third, I see a society in which parenthood does not have to be a *totally* all or nothing proposition. Many of our attitudes about parenthood keep us from being able to think creatively about good alternatives to what we are now doing.

Many people who don't want full-time responsibility for children are loving people who like and enjoy children. Some of them have worked hard to insure that there are children in their lives. They have offered to baby-sit with their friends' children for extended periods, even during two-week vacations. They have made themselves available for emergency child care. And they have realized that sometimes their friends simply need a rest, time to relax or to renew their relationships with their mates. A few nonparents have been lucky enough to have nieces or nephews living close enough to make loving, involved relationships possible.

People with children, on the other hand, often find that they could use just those kinds of help, but no one is available. All their friends have children. Their families may be too far away. And they can't hire a babysitter for two weeks.

If you are interested in having children in your life, you can probably find friends who will offer to leave their children with you sometimes. They will welcome having inexpensive, loving caretakers for their children. Many people are already sharing children through this type of informal arrangement. And the children benefit, too. They get to know adults other than their parents or teachers, adults who can be their friends.

Perhaps those of us who consider never having children do so because we ask something else of life. That something else is harder to identify, to pin down. Sometimes I yearn to be like the old-time Vermonters who took life as it came, rocks in their fields, babies in their cradles. Asking for nothing, giving all they had to the care of the land and their families, they lived without questioning the return. I feel a little envious, a little ashamed when I think about them. Who am I to have this luxury of questioning, this abundance of directions?

Yet a wise voice within me says that envy is useless, shame unnecessary. Other pathways need to be followed; life both gives and takes in different ways. We each must choose, at every fork, to take one road and leave the other untaken. Choice, it seems, is our modern blessing—and our curse.

People who choose not to have children are making a legitimate choice, one that makes a contribution to the rest of society. Respect that choice. Trust those who have made it. They don't need your approval, but they could use your acceptance.

Many ways of life are possible today. Choose the one that keeps you true to yourself.

Suggestions for Further Reading

T HE BOOKS AND ARTICLES listed here are only a sampling of what is available in these areas: the childfree alternative, the psychology and sociology of childbearing, and the effects of population on other social issues. I have listed those which were helpful to me in putting this book together and some which cover areas not included here. For a complete bibliography and for information on making decisions about parenthood, write:

> National Alliance for Optional Parenthood
> 3 North Liberty Street
> Baltimore, Maryland 21201
> (301) 752-7456

In addition, couples who are seeking professional help in making a decision about parenthood should be aware that their counselor can obtain the Optional Parenthood Questionnaire. It is a tool developed to help people explore their feelings and thoughts about parenthood. Anyone can order it, but it was specifically designed to be used in a counseling situation; an interpretation manual is available. (Order it from the National Alliance for Optional Parenthood at the address given above.)

175

This organization will also provide help in planning and conducting workshops on making decisions about parenthood.

I recently found an excellent bibliography on many aspects of parenting, including the decision whether or not to become one. *Parenting, An Annotated Bibliography*, was prepared by the National Center on Child Abuse and Neglect, Department of Health, Education and Welfare. It is DHEW Publication No. (OHDS) 78-30134. Write the DHEW, Washington, D.C. 20201.

Andorka, Rudolf. *Determinants of Fertility in Advanced Societies.* New York: Free Press, 1978.

Anthony, E. James and Benedek, Therese. *Parenthood: Its Psychology and Psychopathology.* Boston: Little, Brown, and Co., 1970.

Bernard, Jessie. *The Future of Marriage.* New York: World Publishing, 1972.

Bernard, Jessie. *The Future of Motherhood.* New York: The Dial Press, 1974.

Blake, J. "Reproductive Motivation and Population Policy." In *Population: A Clash of Prophets,* edited by E. Pohlman. New York: New American Library, 1973.

Ehrlich, Paul. *The Population Bomb.* New York: Ballantine Books, 1968.

Farber, S. and R. Wilson, eds. "The Unmothered Woman." In *The Challenge to Women.* New York: Basic Books, 1966.

Group for the Advancement of Psychiatry. *The Joys and Sorrows of Parenthood.* New York: Scribners, 1975.

LeMasters, E. E. "Parenthood as Crisis." *Marriage and Family Living.* Vol. 19, No. 4. November, 1957.

Mead, Margaret. "Trial Parenthood." *Redbook.* June, 1973.

Meadows, Dennis, et al. *The Limits to Growth.* Washington, D.C.: Potomac Association, 1972.

Peck, Ellen and Senderowitz, Judith. *Pronatalism, the Myth of Mom and Apple Pie.* New York: T. Crowell and Co., 1974.

Peck, Ellen. *The Baby Trap.* New York: Pinnacle Books, 1971.

Pohlman, Edward. "Childlessness, Intentional and Unintentional: Psychological and Social Aspects." *Journal of Nervous and Mental Diseases.* Vol. 151, No. 1. 1970.

Schlesinger, Benjamin. *One-Parent Family: Perspectives and Annotated Bibliography.* 4th Ed. Toronto: University of Toronto Press, 1979.

Silverman, Anna and Arnold. *The Case Against Having Children.* New York: David McKay Co., Inc., 1971.

Tapinos, Georges Photios. *Six Billion People: Demographic Dilemmas and World Politics* (Council on Foreign Relations, 1980's Project). New York: McGraw-Hill, 1978.

U.S. Commission on Civil Rights. *Constitutional Aspects of the Right to Limit Childbearing.* Washington, D.C.: U.S. Govt. Printing Office. April, 1975.

U.S. Commission on Population Growth and the American Future. *Population and the American Future,* a report. New York: New American Library, Inc., 1972.

Veevers, J. E. *Childless by Choice.* Toronto: Gage Educational Publishers, 1975.

Whelan, Elizabeth M. *A Baby . . . Maybe: A Guide to Making the Most Fateful Decision of Your Life.* New York: Bobbs Merrill and Co., Inc., 1975.

Williams, Elizabeth. *Notes of a Feminist Therapist.* New York: Dell, 1977.